WORKERS' EDUCATION

AT THE

UNIVERSITY LEVEL

When I look back on the processes of history, when I survey the genesis of America, I see this written over every page: that the nations are renewed from the bottom, not from the top; that the genius which springs up from the ranks of unknown men is the genius which renews the youth and energy of the people. Everything I know about history, every bit of experience and observation that has contributed to my thought, has confirmed me in the conviction that the real wisdom of human life is compounded out of the experiences of ordinary men. The utility, the vitality, the fruitage of life does not come from the top to the bottom; it comes, like the natural growth of a great tree, from the soil, up through the trunk into the branches to the foliage and the fruit. The great struggling unknown masses of the men who are at the base of everything are the dynamic force that is lifting the levels of society. A nation is as great, and only as great, as her rank and file.

— WOODROW WILSON

Workers' Education at the University Level

by Irvine L. H. Kerrison

Rutgers University Press
New Brunswick, N.J.
1951

Copyright 1951 by the Trustees of Rutgers College
in New Jersey. All Rights Reserved

Manufactured in the United States of America

To my father, Herbert Reginald Kerrison

Preface

It is my sincere hope that this book will prove useful to workers' education specialists, adult educators in other fields, college and university administrators who are anxious to serve the educational needs of the total community, and general readers who wish to keep in touch with developments in adult education.

Space will not permit me to list all of my colleagues in workers' and adult education who have aided me in one way or another. However, I feel bound to thank several persons who have been especially helpful.

I am indebted to Professors Wilbur C. Hallenbeck, Edmund deS. Brunner and Karl W. Bigelow of Teachers College, Columbia University, for critical analysis of the manuscript. Norman C. Miller, retired dean, Rutgers University College and Extension, has made available essential original material and, from his pioneering experience, a fund of information on workers' education activities of the National University Extension Association. I owe much to my secretary, Mrs. Coralie G. Farlee, who typed and checked the manuscript in its several stages of development. The criticisms and suggestions of Miss Page Spencer, Associate Editor, Rutgers University Press, have been most valuable.

Finally, I should like to thank my wife, Eleanor Rothfuss Kerrison, for her sound counsel, patience and forbearance. Without wives like her, books by professors would never be written.

I. L. H. K.

New Brunswick, New Jersey
September, 1951

Table of Contents

INTRODUCTION xi

1 Need for College and University Workers' Education . . 3

2 Problems Facing College and University Workers' Education 27

3 Organization and Administration of College and University Workers' Education 44

4 College and University Workers' Education Programs Today 62

5 Trends in College and University Workers' Education . . 88

6 Areas of Operation for College and University Workers' Education 104

7 Functional Approach to College and University Workers' Education 118

8 Essentials of an Effective Functional College and University Workers' Education Program 131

BIBLIOGRAPHY 146

APPENDIX I. Survey questionnaire: current experiences of colleges and universities in workers' education 156

APPENDIX II. List of colleges and universities surveyed . 166

APPENDIX III. Workers' education directors cooperating in exchange of materials 170

APPENDIX IV. First summer institute, International Chemical Workers Union–AFL . . . 172

INDEX 175

Introduction
by Mark Starr[1]

Workers' education is slowly but surely securing deserved attention and this book is further valuable evidence of that welcome development to replace previous neglect.

In 1941 *Workers' Education in the United States* was published, with Theodore Brameld as editor. Later Caroline Ware made a study in *Labor Education in Universities* which aroused considerable interest. The University of Chicago has sponsored a recent book, *Union Leadership Training*, by Alexander A. Liveright, to help in preparation of union leaders. There have been scattered pamphlets, articles and reprints from learned journals describing, criticizing and praising the efforts of colleges in this field.

In New York State, Cornell University has created a special school for the study of industrial and labor relations which offers a four-year course based upon the principle of joint study by Labor and Management. Unions have sent some of their representatives to Harvard on Labor Fellowships. Dr. Kerrison's book makes a valuable survey of what other colleges have done.

Meanwhile the International Ladies' Garment Workers' Union, dissatisfied with the training facilities provided by the previous efforts, has set up its own Training Institute, with guaranteed jobs and union membership for the men and women who successfully undertake one year's work composed of theoretical studies and practical field work in union administration.

Thus in the decade 1941–51 there have been many experiments in

1. Educational Director, International Ladies' Garment Workers' Union.

establishing relations between our institutions of higher learning and trade unions whose members need adequate and proper workers' education commensurate with the current power and responsibility of organized labor.

Irvine L. H. Kerrison in this book examines in a very capable way some of the ideas, problems and agencies which have arisen in this period of experimentation: Should the universities provide wholetime study courses for union members? Must they be content with part-time study courses carried on in the evening and located in the union hall or in some available local classroom? What methods have been and should be used to recruit the workers and give them confidence in the university's capacity to meet their educational needs? What are those needs and their order of priority? How should such plans be initiated to secure the active participation of the union leaders and members without which all the best laid educational plans are most likely to go astray? What problems will arise when *education* about controversial subjects will look like *propaganda* to opposing partisans, and when vested interests flinch from a fearless and frank scrutiny of their preserves? It is such questions as these which Dr. Kerrison helps us to answer. From practical experience he describes how cooperation can operate to the mutual benefit of the trade union, the university, and the community. Surely, such cooperation will save much of the union activity from sterility and much college study from futility.

The publication of this book with similar documents indicates the progress which workers' education has made in community acceptance in recent years. No one ever questions the need for training the doctor, the teacher, the preacher, the lawyer. Men go through college in order to learn how to be good bond salesmen and to make effective talks in selling insurance policies. So much of education at all levels is devoted to the maintenance and perpetuation of the *status quo* that our mental health can be retained only if groups organized of people interested in making social changes by consent are recognized as agencies worthy of cooperation and assistance. Surely, it is as necessary for labor leaders and trade union activists to secure appropriate knowledge about their group problems and the skills to solve them as it is for men and women to be trained for their important professions in medicine, the law and science. We have learned so little about human engineering and group incentives, we have experimented to such a small extent in understanding human relations in the complexity of groups which compose our modern community, that any presentation of education of, by, and for organized workers, such as Dr. Kerrison has so ably made, is worthy of the consideration of all thoughtful members of our community.

He is fully aware of the failure which has come to certain attempts in cooperation between the universities and organized labor as a result of the neglect of the specific needs of the trade unions and, consequently, a handicap of suspicion reinforced by the cumulative effect of past neglect.

From personal experience, he can describe the slow and difficult path which sometimes must be followed before mutual trust is established. There is the hangover, the cultural lag, because actually some university professors unconsciously have been "chaplains on the pirate ship" of exploitation, some of their students have been scabs in strikes, and some of their learned treatises have been in effect a rationalization of unrestricted greed and plausible defenses of social injustice and out-moded institutions and customs. However, those days are passing, and colleges, particularly those which depend upon the public support, are beginning to recognize workers' education as their responsibility. Of the 42 million men and women who work for wages and salaries in the United States, 35 per cent are now organized in trade unions. With that power of organized labor has come the responsibility to use it wisely both in economic and in political action and for short term and long term goals. Trade union members are an important section of the community, and they cannot be ignored.

The basic assumption of democratic living is equality of opportunity and access to information. Give the people the light and they will surely find the way, is the presumption of all who believe in the great principles upon which this Republic is founded. Surely, organized education should be at pains to create a fair and equal access to all helpful information. But more than information is needed. Dr. Kerrison's book is valuable because he has the imagination to see the great potentiality of further and effective education in social science by which we can overcome our social illiteracy in industrial and international relations and equate our technical knowledge and skills with social understanding.

WORKERS' EDUCATION

AT THE

UNIVERSITY LEVEL

1

Need for College and University Workers' Education

TRADE UNIONS ARE AWAKening to the fact that they have a strategic function to perform in American life. Labor leaders realize that union members must come to understand the economic, political and social forces at work in present-day society and must be prepared to enter new areas of social action and social responsibility. Unions are reorienting themselves toward active participation in the full life of the nation. One indication is to be found in the work of the community service departments of both AFL and CIO.

In 1942, labor participated in community service programs in only ninety localities. A recent report of the CIO Community Services Committee states that unions are officially represented on more than 7,000 community service programs throughout the nation. Within the last decade, labor has become increasingly an integral part of the American community service program. Union leaders now serve as board members of Community Chests and the Boy Scouts and as advisors to family service agencies and public assistance programs.

Because of community service work, David Dubinsky probably is better known today than a powerful banker like Winthrop Aldrich with whom he serves on the United Negro College Fund. Robert Dingwell, president of a UAW–CIO local in Michigan, serves without pay on several of Lansing's civic commissions. Across America, from Dubinsky to Dingwell, unionism serves the American community and is winning new respect thereby.[1]

Labor needs many more individuals who are qualified to take part in this important work. And behind these men and women there is urgent need for trained union officers and enlightened organized workers.

The obligations and duties of labor leaders and union members have multiplied many times over during the past two decades. As Fannia Cohn, one of the pioneers in American workers' education, points out, "If enlightened democracy is to prevail in a union, the membership must be capable of intelligently choosing its leadership." The leaders themselves "must be prepared emotionally and intellectually to take advantage of every opportunity that will strengthen the union [they] represent and thus add to the strength of the labor movement as a whole, the industry in which [they are] engaged and the community in which [they] live."[2]

Workers' education increasingly is becoming the vehicle by which union officers are trained and organized workers are enlightened. At no time in labor's past was it needed as urgently as it is today.

Organizing the unorganized still is the major task confronting American unions. Many of the large unions in this country are in their early teens. None of them has yet graduated enough leaders from officers' candidate school; none of them has yet put enough rank-and-file cadres through basic training in the fundamentals of trade unionism. Most American unions need additional leaders, particularly in second-line positions; most American unions need additional seasoned rank-and-filers as a steadying influence at the local union level.

Demand is growing throughout the labor movement for instruction in utilitarian "tool" subjects like collective bargaining, public

---

1. Daniel Bell, "The Worker and His Civic Function," *Monthly Labor Review*, 71:68, July, 1950.
2. Fannia M. Cohn, *Why Workers' Education?* (New York: International Ladies' Garment Workers Union Educational Department, 1948), p. 2.

speaking, parliamentary procedure, and time study. The satisfaction of this demand alone is a task far beyond the resources of the labor movement itself.

The job that must be done is of such tremendous magnitude that the help of colleges and universities, particularly those under public control, simply has to be enlisted. Educators and union leaders are aware of this fact.

In 1938, the President's Advisory Committee on Education underscored the importance of the role of institutions of higher learning in workers' education.

> If an intelligent labor movement is essential to democratic progress, then education of labor leaders is as important as education of financiers and engineers. The failure of colleges and universities to maintain departments for the higher education of workers is from the standpoint of democracy little less than a calamity.[3]

And two years later, T. R. Adam, in his analysis of the social significance of workers' education, pointed out with specifics the fact that workers' education is the business of the community and that university extension service is in the forefront of possible state instrumentalities for carrying on workers' education. The original objective of university extension, he said, was to free sources of learning imprisoned within colleges and universities and to spread that learning over as wide as possible an area. As part of the process, it has lately recovered workers' education as a major part of its function.[4]

To be added to the opinions of educational authorities is the cold fact of the size and growing strength of the American labor movement. Unions now have a membership of over 16,000,000 Americans — approximately one half of all production and clerical workers in industries in which unions make a serious attempt to organize all such workers. As University of Wisconsin Professor Edwin Witte says:

> Of all organizations concerned with economic matters, they have by far the largest constituency. Clearly such a large group

---

3. Quoted in Frank E. Baker, "Relations with Public Education: An Overview of the Issues," *Fifth Yearbook of the John Dewey Society* (New York: Harper and Brothers, Publishers, 1941), pp. 247-48.
4. T. R. Adam, *The Worker's Road to Learning* (New York: American Association for Adult Education, 1940), pp. 144-46.

of citizens are entitled to get service from the universities on the same basis as are other groups in our society.[5]

Creation of workers' education programs, particularly within industrial relations institutes, and appropriation of state funds for the support of these programs, increasingly observable since 1944, indicate that more than a few university administrators and those to whom they are responsible are developing in their understanding of the need and are taking action to meet it.

With few exceptions, both labor leaders and the educational technicians employed by them support this development in the universities, because they realize that the task of educating today's union membership is overwhelming. It presents a problem of adult education with little organized subject matter and without adequate teaching staffs. While it is increasing in volume and quality, workers' education material emanating from union education departments is still pitifully inadequate. The educational departments of both the AFL and the CIO are undermanned and overworked. Most international unions, AFL or CIO, have one man education departments. Moreover, in most instances, that one man performs a double function: in addition to being responsible for the union's education program, he usually is its publicity or research director.

The inevitable conclusion is that, while union-financed education departments will continue and in some cases expand their work, an adequate program of workers' education nationwide in scope will remain beyond the resources of the labor movement itself. The reasonable expectation should therefore be that college and university workers' education programs backed by increased public aid, both state and federal, will carry an ever enlarging share of the load. Paul Essert, Director of Columbia University's Institute of Adult Education, lends weight to this expectation in saying that both management and labor increasingly will require assistance in the application of teaching methods and industrial research to their programs. According to Essert, both sides of the bargaining table will depend upon and urge colleges and universities to provide not only the narrow specializations such as supervisory skill training and effective trade

---

5. Edwin F. Witte, "The University and Labor Education," (unpublished paper read before the University-Labor Education Conference, Washington, May 28, 1947), p. 17.

unionism, but also broader discussion of the economic, social and political issues confronting them.[6]

To secure training that will enable them to perform their duties with both dispatch and credit, workers and those union officials charged with workers' education projects especially look to tax-supported institutions of higher learning for the same educational opportunities now offered by those institutions through agricultural, business, engineering and other colleges and departments offering specialized professional or skill training. Statements of AFL and CIO educational leaders point up this quest.

Spencer Miller, Jr., before he left the directorship of the Workers Education Bureau, strongly reiterated his belief that workers' education would develop closer ties with institutions of higher learning. Cooperation would develop "where they can collaborate most effectively in the promotion of workers' education, but it will extend to a far larger area of cooperative endeavor."[7] Miller's successor, John D. Connors, confirms that belief, salting it with a word of caution. While he is sure that college and university workers' education can help develop a democratic trade union movement and, on occasion, forestall labor disputes, Connors wants it understood that "labor does not consider these university-sponsored programs a panacea for all of labor's problems."[8]

In 1947, Kermit Eby, then CIO director of education and research, stated that union resources were too limited to satisfy labor's demand for educational programs, and added that "as American universities and colleges show interest in labor education, union educational directors are turning toward their doors."[9] Exercising caution similar to that displayed by Connors, George Guernsey, present CIO associate director of education, while asserting that there are "several lines of cooperation along which the CIO and university groups might

6. Paul L. Essert, "Adult Education in the United States: A Report on General and Institutional Trends Based on an Extended Tour of the Nation in 1947–1948" (unpublished report to Teachers College, Columbia University, New York, 1948), p. 14. This report has been incorporated into Dr. Essert's recently published *Creative Leadership of Adult Education* (New York: Prentice-Hall, Inc., 1951), 339 pp.
7. Spencer Miller, Jr., "Retrospect and Forecast in Workers' Education," *Journal of Adult Education*, 8:345–46, June, 1936.
8. John D. Connors, *Workers' Education: What? Why? How?* (New York: Workers Education Bureau of America, 1947), p. 12.
9. Kermit Eby and Frank Fernbach, "Unions Look at Education in Industrial Relations," *Journal of Educational Sociology*, 20:495, April, 1947.

work for the expansion of labor education programs,"[10] also says: "In many cases, we find programs being offered which do not meet the needs of the labor movement."[11]

With more assurance, Emery F. Bacon, education specialist with the United Steelworkers of America–CIO, urges the National University Extension Association to strengthen and expand the program of its committee on workers' education:

> I say this because I believe labor education is impossible without using the facilities of the university and cooperating closely with it. . . . Unions have tried to solve the problem for many years within their own ranks. Because of fear, suspicion or union politics, rarely have unions sought the answer where the answer can be found. The problem can only be solved by educational specialists dealing with workers' groups first hand.[12]

The Steelworkers have acted assiduously on this belief. No other international union carries on as large a program with institutions of higher learning. The union's officers feel that it is fortunate that there are "great people's universities and private colleges scattered across our land which are interested in aiding Unions to help train their people . . ."[13]

In addition to this general support given college- and university-conducted workers' education, specific support to local programs is given by statewide labor groups. For example, all three statewide trade union organizations in New Jersey endorse their state university's service to labor.[14]

The survey on which much of this work is based demonstrates that labor endorsements have been given in many another state where colleges and universities are carrying on workers' education programs.

10. George T. Guernsey, "The Education Program of the National CIO: Possible Lines of Cooperation with Universities" (unpublished paper read before University-Labor Education Conference, U.S. Department of Labor, Washington, May 29, 1947), p. 1.
11. *Ibid.*, p. 6.
12. Quoted in J. B. M. Arthur, "Report of the Recorder: Industrial Relations and Workers' Education Section Meeting" (unpublished report section of meeting of National University Extension Association, Chicago, May 4–5, 1948), p. 12.
13. *Educational Classes in Your Local Union: A Joint Union-University Program* (Pittsburgh: United Steelworkers of America, 1949), p. 3.
14. *Your State University Provides: An Answer to Labor's Educational Needs* (New Brunswick, New Jersey: Institute of Management and Labor Relations, Rutgers University, 1950), p. 9.

They testify to the enthusiasm with which such programs have been greeted by top labor officials.

These statements are important, too, in another sense. They confirm the fact that adult education for industrial workers is not a matter of temporary interest. It is not merely a movement attempting to make up for the education the worker may have lost when compelled to enter industry at an early age, but it is a movement which has become a permanent element of our national educational effort. This workers' education activity stresses the concept that education is a continuous lifetime process and that adult education is as much a part of democratic living as is the preparation of youth for adult life.

The American worker seeks knowledge and understanding, not diplomas and degrees. The institutions of higher learning surveyed, especially state and municipal universities which derive their support from the people, increasingly are discovering that they cannot justify a position of indifference toward the workers' education that labor is demanding.

Not all colleges and universities are indifferent to this demand. Some American institutions of higher learning, because they have long been interested in adult education, have been attempting to help satisfy workers' needs for over a century.

American workers' education is a specialized branch of adult education conducted for an homogeneous segment of society and has problems of its own. From its earliest days it has played an important role in the development of American adult education at the university level, which has its roots in the mechanics' institutes of the early nineteenth century.[15] The English system of university extension, to which workers' education owes so much, was first vigorously advocated for the United States in 1887, largely as a result of a successful Workingman's Institute conducted by Johns Hopkins University at Canton, Maryland, in 1879.[16]

Today, workers' education is a growing part of the mushrooming and well integrated university extension movement which operates within the framework of the National University Extension Association.

15. James Creese, *The Extension of University Teaching* (New York: American Association for Adult Education, 1941), pp. 25–26.
16. *Ibid.*, pp. 37–49.

The NUEA includes in its membership most of the larger institutions of higher learning that have well established extension programs. Since its establishment in 1915, seventy-one colleges and universities have joined NUEA. Their purpose is set forth as follows:

> . . . the maintenance of an official and authorized organization through which colleges and universities engaged in educational extension work may confer for the development and the promotion of the best ideals, methods and standards.
>
> Membership includes state universities, members of the Association of American Universities, institutions on the approved list of the Association of American Universities and other institutions which maintain adequate extension programs meeting NUEA standards.[17]

The National University Extension Association has a standing committee on workers' education. Thus there is a medium for developing relationships between organized workers' education and organized university adult education.

But long before there was any established American workers' education movement and long before the establishment of NUEA, cordial relationships were developing between unions and individual college professors. From the first instances of American labor-conducted workers' education, unions have drawn upon the resources of colleges and universities by securing faculty members as instructors and lecturers.[18]

More formal and thoroughly organized relationships between unions and universities in the United States got their impetus soon after World War I when the University of California initiated an unusual workers' education program the year prior to the birth of the organized American workers' education movement.

In 1920, a director of workers' education was appointed by the University of California's Extension Division. His job, created in response to numerous requests from labor groups, encompassed first a survey of the feasibility of a workers' education program in the state and the setting up of experimental classes. Survey and classes indicated that both the rank and file and its representatives would

---

17. *Proceedings of the Thirty-Fourth Annual Meeting of the National University Extension Association at Edgewater Gulf Hotel, Edgewater Park, Mississippi, May 2–5, 1949* (Bloomington, Indiana: Feltus Printing Company, Inc., 1949), pp. 11–12.

18. John D. Connors, "A New Frontier: Workers' Education and the University," *Adult Education Journal*, 5:73–7, April, 1946.

Need for University Program

benefit from educational activities conducted under the joint auspices of the university and the California State Federation of Labor. It was decided to go ahead with the effort and control was placed in the hands of a committee composed of five members representing labor and four the university.[19]

Over a sixteen-year period this program held eight summer schools, each of four weeks' duration and each enrolling from fifty to sixty persons. In addition, about a hundred and fifty classes in labor history, labor economics, labor law, English, public speaking, and history were conducted. And over five hundred talks and discussions on a host of subjects were taken to local union groups.[20]

The program lives on today within the framework of the university's Institute of Industrial Relations which maintains centers on both Berkeley and Los Angeles campuses.

The California experiment soon was supplemented by other workers' education activity at the college and university level, for 1921 marks the beginnings of the first organized American workers' education movement. Among signal achievements that year were the creation of the Workers Education Bureau of America, first sessions of the Bryn Mawr Summer School for Women Workers in Industry, and the organization of Brookwood Labor College.

The Workers Education Bureau came into being when a number of men and women connected with the trade union movement met in New York City in April, 1921, with a vision of creating an agency for the advancement of workers' education. They had as their aim the development of an educational arm for labor that would promote neither sects nor "isms." Many of them were either familiar with or experienced in the British Workers' Educational Association, and part of their aim was to work out relationships with institutions of higher learning.

The Bryn Mawr Summer School for Women Workers in Industry was designed as a cooperative venture between college women and women in industry. Its purpose was to hasten the educational emancipation of women, just as the nineteenth amendment the year before had hastened their political emancipation. Its founders had the coun-

---

19. John L. Kerchen, "California Plan Expanded on Pacific Coast," *Journal of Adult Education*, 6:521, October, 1934.
20. *Proceedings of the Twenty-Second Annual Convention of the National University Extension Association at Washington University, St. Louis, Missouri, May 13–15, 1937* (Spencer, Indiana: Samuel M. Guard and Co., Inc., Printers, 1937), p. 62.

sel and advice of the Women's Trade Union League on specific program, and the services of Hilda W. Smith, today as then one of the top figures in American workers' education, as director.

Brookwood Labor College was conceived by a small group of pioneers, many of them the same people who founded the Workers Education Bureau, who believed that adult American workers would leave their jobs and homes, without the offer of financial advancement as an incentive, to do serious study in a resident college.

These developments in workers' education were being closely watched by colleges and universities. In 1922, J. C. Egbert, then Director of Extension at Columbia University, urged the National University Extension Association, Lexington, Kentucky, convention to work with labor groups. He knew that much of the initiative of the 1921 upsurge had come from people within the university ranks. Several important colleges and universities either were already working with labor groups or took Director Egbert's advice.

The informally organized trade union colleges of the early twenties received much assistance from colleges and universities. For example, the Trade Union College of Boston was aided materially by not one but three prominent schools — Harvard, the Massachusetts Institute of Technology, and Tufts College.[21]

During this same period, Amherst and Bryn Mawr colleges established joint administrative committees for the promotion of adult education of industrial workers.

Direct extension service to labor was initiated by Syracuse University which, in 1922, conducted a sixteen-session class in economics for workers. Most of the eighty students who enrolled were trade union officers.[22]

A few classes for workers in economics, sociology and psychology were conducted at Woodward High School, Cincinnati, in the same and in the following year. These classes were held under the joint auspices of the Central Labor Council and the University of Cincinnati.[23]

These and other experiments in union-university cooperation in

21. *Proceedings of the National University Extension Association at Lexington, Kentucky, April 20, 21, 22, 1922* (Boston: Wright and Potter Printing Company, 1922), p. 58.
22. *Ibid.*, p. 52.
23. "Workers' Education" (unpublished report prepared by Special Committee of the National University Extension Association, Madison, Wisconsin, May, 1924), p. 10.

Need for University Program

the field of workers' education prompted Norman C. Miller, then of Pennsylvania State College, to offer a resolution at the 1923 National University Extension Association convention. Miller asked for the appointment of a committee representing all sections of the country to study the probable results of teaching workers' education subjects in colleges and universities. The resolution was approved; a committee was appointed. As a result of the convention report of this committee the following year, the NUEA set up a standing committee on workers' education which still is functioning.[24]

Miller, in writing the report of the committee, concluded that "the consensus of opinion seems to be that the ultimate results of such courses . . . would be of good benefit both to the institution and to the labor bodies as well as to industry in general."[25]

At the same 1923 convention, NUEA passed a resolution confirming its belief that university extension is primarily an instrument for the promotion of adult education in universities and affirming its eagerness to cooperate with workers' education agencies like the Workers Education Bureau.[26] The following year, it was even more pronounced in its support of workers' education, strongly urging all of its members to cooperate with workers and organized labor groups wherever possible.[27]

But despite all urging, despite activities in the field of colleges and universities and within the labor movement itself, by 1925 James H. Maurer, a prominent labor leader and president of the WEB, was forced to admit the failure of the 1921 movement in which he had been a pioneer and leader. Even the sanction given by the AFL when it took over the WEB in 1923 had not been enough to keep the movement vigorous.

Growing apathy among union members and growing cynicism among union leaders, the product of industry's "open shop" drive, was responsible for this collapse. The labor movement was too busy fighting for survival to be concerned about larger ideas and purposes.

---

24. *Proceedings of the Eighth Annual Conference National University Extension Association at St. Louis, Missouri, April 19, 20, 21, 1923* (Boston: Wright and Potter Printing Company, 1923), p. 59.
25. Norman C. Miller, "Report of Study for the National University Extension Association on the Matter of Cooperation Between State Institutions and Trade Union Bodies together with a Series of Letters from Prominent Industrial and Business Leaders Dealing with the Subject" (unpublished report, 1924), p. 1.
26. "Workers' Education," *op. cit.*, p. 1.
27. *Ibid.*, p. 23.

Only in rare instances did large and active programs of workers' education continue.

Within the university field, continued belief in the value of workers' education prevailed. The report of the 1927 National University Extension Association workers' education committee indicated that its members would continue to push workers' education both as a phase of adult education and as a stage in the evolution of modern industrial society.[28] Typical of reactions of forward-looking university people was that of NUEA president James A. Moyer, speaking before the organization's 1928 annual meeting. Moyer, who then was with the Massachusetts Department of Education, said:

> I can see no better use for the endowed funds of the great Eastern universities than to provide entirely at the expense of the institution the services of one or two of their best and most popular teachers to give classes in subjects which may be requested by the representatives of a trade union college in a nearby city.[29]

In the Southwest, in 1929, a prominent university was conducting a workers' education program. The University of Oklahoma Extension Division held labor problems classes for bakers, bricklayers, plumbers and painters, and a social evolution class for electricians that year. Both the Oklahoma State Federation of Labor and local central labor councils cooperated to make the offerings successful.[30]

In 1931, Rutgers University pioneered with a labor institute which set a pattern since followed in thirty-seven other states. Partly because of his familiarity with the Workers Educational Association, which he had observed during trips to Britain, and partly because of a strong desire to have the university do what it could to ameliorate the effects of the 1929 collapse, Norman C. Miller, then head of extension at Rutgers, conceived the idea of a short on-campus resident institute for workers to study the problem of unemployment.

He took his idea to Spencer Miller, Jr., and to Arthur Quinn, at

---

28. *Proceedings of the National University Extension Association at Chapel Hill, North Carolina, April 25, 26, 27, 1927* (Boston: Wright and Potter Printing Company, 1925), p. 179.

29. *Proceedings of the National University Extension Association at Lawrence, Kansas, April 25, 26, 27, 1928* (Indianapolis: Wm. B. Burford Printing Company, 1928), p. 23.

30. *Proceedings of the National University Extension Association at Austin, Texas, May 13, 14, 15, 1929* (Bloomington, Indiana: Indiana University Press, 1929), p. 179.

Need for University Program   15

that time president of the New Jersey State Federation of Labor. Both men soon shared Miller's enthusiasm, the Rutgers trustees approved the plan, the New Jersey State Federation of Labor concurred, and the Rutgers Labor Institute was born.

That first institute was so successful that the convention of the state federation voted to make the institute an annual affair. Each year the institute, built around one great issue of the day, is planned and executed by a joint committee on which representatives of the New Jersey State Federation of Labor, the Workers Education Bureau–AFL and the State University serve. June, 1950, marked the twentieth anniversary celebration of this successful enterprise in union-university cooperation in the field of workers' education.

Another milestone for workers' education is the year 1933 when Franklin D. Roosevelt and the New Deal began to dominate the national scene. Workers learned that the rights to organize and to bargain collectively were being strengthened and enforced. It was only natural that, in such a climate, there should be a revival of activity in workers' education.

New Deal policies meant the rise of many new unions and the expansion of many of the older ones. In addition, the federal government made direct and positive entry into the field of workers' education via the Work Projects Administration, training ground of so many present leaders in the movement in the United States.

During the mid-thirties, unions uniformly felt the need of assimilating new, inexperienced members, the necessity for making them "union-conscious." The workers' education projects of WPA offered education free to those unions which wanted it. And it was a university person, Hilda W. Smith, of Bryn Mawr College and the Affiliated Schools for Workers, who was chosen to head up these projects.

Beginning about 1935 were the great organizing drives which doubled the size of the labor movement. By 1938 over thirty-five new international unions and organizing committees had been chartered. Union education departments and colleges and universities worked with the WPA workers' education projects to provide educational services of all kinds for this vast mass of newly organized labor. Some idea of the aims and scope of the program was given by L. R. Alderman, WPA Education Director, in speaking to the 1936 annual meeting of the National University Extension Association.

Workers' education offers to men and women workers in industry, business, commerce, domestic service and other occupations an opportunity to train themselves in clear thinking through the study of those questions closely related to their daily lives as workers and as citizens. The instruction program is based on an attitude of scientific inquiry in the light of all the facts, and implies complete freedom of teaching and discussion. Its purpose is to stimulate an active and continued interest in the economic problems of our times and to develop a sense of responsibility for their solution. Included as part of the emergency program in general adult education, classes for industrial and rural workers have been carried on for the past two years with unemployed teachers in thirty states.[31]

Progress under the WPA projects was steady but not nearly as expansive as the enormous growth of the labor movement would seem to warrant. Then, as the war clouds began to bank in Europe, jobs became plentiful, wages and conditions were good, and payment for overtime was sufficiently high to make all but the most interested worker indifferent to both the value and the offerings of American workers' education.

But, as had happened before, relapse was followed by rally.

Toward the end of World War II, beginning particularly in 1944, colleges and universities emphasized renewed interest in workers' education. State legislatures began to give substantial grants to a number of industrial relations and labor-management institutes established at state colleges and state universities, which, as part of their function, were to carry on programs in workers' education. Private institutions, both religious and non-sectarian, to a lesser degree began to finance workers' education activities.

This increased college and university participation is the most striking development in workers' education in recent years. In a few cases, at the University of Michigan for example, institutions of higher learning entered the field to operate programs geared solely to trade union needs. In other cases, workers' education activity exists within the broader framework of an industrial relations center or institute. The result has been that college and university programs

---

31. *Proceedings of the Twenty-First Annual Convention of the National University Extension Association at The Louisiana State University, Baton Rouge, Louisiana, May 7–9, 1936* (Indianapolis: Wm. B. Burford Printing Company, 1936), p. 63.

Need for University Program

for workers today are addressed to all levels of the union hierarchy and include on-campus undergraduate and graduate work, extension classes, seminars and conferences, research and the preparation of materials.

Yet, without additional state and federal aid, it is doubtful that the extension work, which is of first priority in labor's eyes, can be sufficiently expanded. Lester Dix, speaking of the Cornell program, says:

> The State School of Industrial and Labor Relations is using courses, but unless it is eventually empowered and encouraged to develop a great field extension program for labor and industry paralleling that for rural life, it may have to turn over the bulk of its course-giving to other agencies simply from pressure of demand upon its resources.[32]

Since the only "other agencies" at the present time, the unions themselves, do not support adequate programs of workers' education, clearly there is a tremendous stake involved in expanding college and university programs.

NUEA sees the necessity in terms of the function of affiliated institutions. In 1944 it noted with approval the "progress that is being made by certain member institutions in developing programs of workers' education."[33] In 1947 it observed that more than one-fourth of the sixty-six institutions of higher learning then affiliated had launched programs either for labor alone or for labor and management, and that over a dozen other association members had programs in the planning stage.[34]

This observation could be made because by 1947 state funds for workers' education programs were available in New York, Michigan, Illinois, California and Rhode Island. In New Jersey a bill for the purpose, subsequently passed, was before the legislature, and other industrial states were showing interest. Since that year a few additional state-financed programs have come into being, but by no means in sufficient numbers to meet the demand for them.

32. Lester Dix, *Higher Education Services to Adult Education in New York State* (University of the State of New York Bulletin No. 1357. Albany, New York: University of the State of New York, December 1, 1948), p. 10.
33. *Proceedings of the Twenty-Ninth Annual Meeting of the National University Extension Association at the Hotel Statler, St. Louis, Missouri, May 3 and 4, 1944* (Bloomington, Indiana: Feltus Printing Company, Inc., 1944), p. 59.
34. *Proceedings of the Thirty-Second Annual Meeting of the National University Extension Association at the Hotel Dennis, Atlantic City, New Jersey, May 6, 7, 8 and 9, 1947* (Bloomington, Indiana: Feltus Printing Company, Inc., 1947), p. 157.

Most of the colleges and universities surveyed have had to draw from the general funds of their institutions to start programs. Almost everywhere financial support for workers' education has been precarious and inadequate. But the significant thing is that financial support increasingly is being found.

Aside from the fact that institutions of higher learning look upon provision of workers' education services as part of their adult education function, there are special reasons why they are in the field and why they are finding money for workers' education.

First, colleges and universities are fast becoming aware that labor's support is important to their total operation. Today labor's voice commands new authority in the formulation of public policy.

Second, as their workers' education program brochures state, many of these institutions believe that by helping the labor movement train its people they will be making a contribution toward the improvement of industrial relations.

Third, there are, regrettably, a few colleges and universities which push a kind of workers' education which is designed to curb union militancy and which is aimed at making unions more "respectable." These mistaken institutions, of course, will have short-lived careers in the field.

No matter how much institutions of higher learning now desire to provide more workers' education activities, without larger funds they cannot expand their offerings to the degree warranted by demand. Funds on the requisite scale means additional state aid and at least the beginnings of federal aid.

Yet throughout its history, workers' education in the United States has had little support from state and federal governments. Workers' education overseas, particularly in England and the Scandinavian countries, has always had strong financial support — local, regional and national.

Spencer Miller, Jr., estimates that of monies spent for workers' education in the United States from 1931 to 1938, unions contributed 38 per cent; WPA, 24 per cent; liberal sympathizers, 20 per cent; foundations, 13 per cent; and state governments 5 per cent.[35] It is evident that, even during the period when government support of

---

35. Quoted in Ernest E. Schwartztrauber, "Administering Workers' Education," *Fifth Yearbook of the John Dewey Society* (New York: Harper and Brothers, Publishers, 1941), p. 206.

Need for University Program

workers' education was greatest, it accounted for less than one-third of the total funds put forward for such activity. Since the termination of the WPA program, the federal government has spent almost nothing for the education of workers.

But there is hope that the situation will change, that the federal government will begin to appropriate funds, perhaps generously, for the education of workers. Paul Essert maintains that huge federal workers' education programs are possible, that a modest program, modeled after early grants-in-aid to agricultural extension, is probable, and that probably colleges and universities will be asked to assume the major responsibility for whatever program is established.[36]

To provide such federal aid to workers' education and to route the aid through institutions of higher learning is the purpose of the labor extension bills which have been before Congress for the past five years.

It was first proposed in 1942 that a bill be introduced in Congress to establish a labor extension service within the United States Department of Labor. The occasion was a White House conference arranged by Mrs. Franklin Delano Roosevelt and attended by leaders from all branches of organized labor. These leaders approved the proposal, and later the same year the plan was endorsed by both AFL and CIO conventions.

Thus an idea that had been discussed at workers' education conferences held all over the country the previous decade was brought to a specific proposal for action. The proposed legislation was not initiated by a small group of influential people meeting in Washington, but came to the fore as the result of a grass roots movement based on interest and need nationwide in scope and developed over a period of many years. College and university people, particularly those who had participated in the workers' education programs conducted during the depression years, as well as labor leaders, were behind it.

Because of the exigencies of war, it was not until 1946 that a bill could be introduced in Congress. That year, Congressmen Andrew Biemiller and Estes Kefauver took the original bills up the Hill to the Seventy-Ninth Congress. These bills expired because Congress adjourned soon after they were introduced.

In 1947 a strengthened and redrafted bill, which had benefited

36. Essert, *op. cit.*, p. 10.

from the advice of interested M. C.'s, arrived in Congress. This bill also contained a number of clauses suggested by the Permanent Committee on Education of the AFL — clauses which had been discussed with and accepted by the CIO and some of the larger independent unions. However, because the Congress had before it what it considered more important legislation, no action was taken.

First action on this revised legislation, reintroduced in the Eightieth Congress, came in 1948. Following sponsorship by Senators Wayne Morse and Elbert D. Thomas and Representatives Ray J. Madden and Thor C. Tollefson, hearings were held before the appropriate Senate and House Committees. Official representatives of all branches of the labor movement testified in favor of the bills as did a number of leading educators, government officials, arbitrators and community leaders. The Senate Committee on Labor and Public Welfare rendered a favorable report. However, the House Committee on Education and Labor took no action before the end of the session.

Undaunted, the many people backing labor extension service presented the proposal to the resolutions committees of both major party conventions. The Democrats included the bill as a plank in their platform.

When the Eighty-First Congress convened in 1949, labor extension service bills were dropped in the hopper in both houses and under bipartisan sponsorship. Five senators, among them George Aiken and Paul Douglas, and fifteen Congressmen introduced bills. Fourteen of the House bills followed the bill already endorsed by all branches of the labor movement. The fifteenth bill, to a substantial degree introduced by Representative Leonard Irving, proposed a plan of administration through the Department of Labor which was favored by the AFL's Permanent Committee on Education. This fifteenth bill, occasioned by AFL reaction to the suspension of the University of Michigan program and the discharge of its director, AFL leader Arthur Elder, may be directly responsible for Congress' failure to date to take further action on labor extension service legislation.

When a widely representative group from the labor movement, from government departments, and from universities, at House hearings held in July, 1949, again urged immediate action on the bill, a number of amendments presented by an AFL representative pointed up differences within the labor movement with regard to the bill

Need for University Program

under discussion. Perhaps it was for this reason that the House committee decided not to vote it out.

President Truman, early in 1950, in both his Message on the State of the Union and his Budget Message, specifically endorsed the labor extension service proposal. But also in January of that year, the House Committee on Education and Labor, meeting in executive session, voted to defer action. It was at that time that Representative Cleveland Bailey, at the request of the AFL, introduced another bill similar to that previously sponsored by his colleague Leonard Irving. The Senate had the bill on its calendar throughout the session but, because of House reluctance to act, passed over it several times.

There is every likelihood that Congress will not act upon the labor extension service proposal until the AFL and the other branches of organized labor can come to some agreement on their differences.

This situation is deplorable because until there is substantial federal appropriation for workers' education, no adequate nationwide program can get under way.

An examination of differences within the labor movement regarding the legislation demonstrates that the controversy is not worthy of the proportions it has assumed.

Essentially, the differences revolve around the method to be used in taking extension services to the field. The AFL supports field offices within the structure of the United States Department of Labor. The labor extension bill establishes centers in each state.

The AFL stated its position in 1949, and reiterated it in 1950:

> . . . the successful efforts of General Motors to destroy a splendid Workers' Education Program at the University of Michigan was further proof that a Labor Extension Service must be a program of the Department of Labor, conducted in cooperation with our trade unions. . . .
>
> . . . For this reason it seems imperative that field offices and demonstration centers be set up at the instance of organized labor groups themselves acting in cooperation with the Department of Labor. In those instances where universities, colleges, or private research agencies may be called in to perform specific services they should be provided on a contract basis under such terms as may be approved by the Department of Labor and the workers making use of such services.[37]

37. *Labor and Education in 1949* (New York: American Federation of Labor, 1950), pp. 16–17; and *Education Program Adapted at the Sixty-Ninth Annual Con-*

The labor extension bill says:

> The Labor Extension Service shall utilize appropriate facilities within the States in carrying out the purposes of this Act. . . .
>
> In order for any State to qualify for funds appropriated under this Act the Governor of such State, after receiving requests for services from bona fide labor organizations State-wide in scope, shall appoint a State labor extension board (hereinafter referred to as the "State board") of at least eight and not more than twelve persons, composed of persons chosen in equal numbers from (1) a panel submitted by bona fide labor organizations State-wide in scope and (2) a panel submitted by cooperating institutions in the State. For the purposes of initial appointments to the State board pursuant to this section, cooperating institutions shall include schools or institutions offering labor extension services.[38]

AFL spokesmen assert that the Department of Labor was set up specifically to foster, promote and develop the welfare of wage earners and should therefore have a more immediate and direct responsibility for the initiation and direction of a labor extension service. Only where the facilities of the Department of Labor are inadequate to provide the services that labor requires should colleges and universities be authorized, by the Labor Department, to handle such services on a contract basis.

This position, of course, is contrary to the whole pattern of public education in the United States. Traditionally, the states have dealt with education. No legislation relating to federal aid for education that did not safeguard this tradition has ever been successfully introduced into Congress.

A plausible explanation of the AFL position is that the federation is so incensed about the unjust treatment of the University of Michigan program that it prefers no bill at all to one which routes funds and services through institutions of higher learning. Such a position fashions a generality out of a specific case. Because one university in one state failed — and in a situation where very special circumstances were operative — AFL members may be deprived of services which they consider essential.

vention of the American Federation of Labor 1950, Houston, Texas, September 18, 1950 (Washington: American Federation of Labor, 1950), p. 9.

38. *Senate Bill No. 110*, Report No. 92, Calendar No. 76, Eighty-First Congress, First Session, introduced January 5, 1949, pp. 4–7.

Need for University Program 23

Actually, the bill opposed by the AFL provides for full representation from the labor movement in the planning and execution of workers' education activities covered by that bill.

In the first place, these activities are designed to broaden and further develop the kind of extension service that has been carried on so successfully through the cooperative effort of farm groups and land grant colleges. But labor extension service will be supplemental rather than duplicative endeavor. And the Department of Labor will be fully involved. The bill states:

> It is declared to be the policy of the Congress that the purpose of this program shall be to enable the Secretary of Labor, in accordance with his duty to promote the welfare of wage earners, through a program for the dissemination of useful knowledge to provide a means by which the Nation may conserve the creative capacities of workers and to promote cooperative relations and mutual understanding between labor and management.[39]

Further, the labor extension service will be established within the Department of Labor and will be charged with providing to bona fide labor organizations, among other things, information on collective bargaining agreements, activities and practices; information and research on the principles and techniques of collective bargaining; information on living and working conditions; and information on labor legislation and the administration of that legislation.

The service will be administered by a director appointed by the President; other employees, subject to civil service laws, will be appointed by the Secretary of Labor. It will be advised by a National Labor Extension Council appointed by the Secretary of Labor and composed of six representatives of bona fide labor organizations and six representatives of cooperating institutions designated by the States.

Certainly, both as regards national administration of the labor extension service and provision of advice to that service, labor's interest seems to be adequately protected.

At the state level, labor participation will be even greater, for the State Board, chosen in equal numbers from labor organizations and cooperating institutions, will administer the service.[40]

39. *Ibid.*, p. 2.
40. *Ibid.*, pp. 7-9.

Nevertheless the position taken by the AFL may completely nullify and has certainly hindered the efforts of the National Committee for the Extension of Labor Education and other proponents of a national labor extension service.

Key groups representing higher education are among these other proponents. The Association of Land Grant Colleges gave the bill its full endorsement. The National University Extension Association endorsed it in principle.

J. O. Keller, assistant to the president at Pennsylvania State College, spoke for NUEA in his capacity as chairman of its Committee on Governmental Information and Action. He testified in Washington on February 18, 1948, before a subcommittee of the Senate Committee on Labor and Public Welfare:

> Our Association is in favor of legislation for adult education and labor education, believing that assistance should be given to all citizens to extend their education, just as the same opportunity is given to the farmer. . . .
>
> Our Association was requested to endorse S 1390 and HR 4332 but our membership in general felt that the provisions of these bills did not permit of our endorsement. The provisions as set forth in the bills do not meet the requirements of a complete adult and labor educational program, nor does the administration of the bills meet with the approval of most of our member institutions.[41]

Keller went on to explain that many NUEA members had workers' education programs which had been developed jointly with organized labor and that, for this reason, state boards as established under the proposed labor extension service bill were unnecessary superfluities. He proclaimed NUEA's belief that federal education subsidies should be channeled solely through public institutions and that the bill as set up did not do that.

It may be that the question of subsidy allocation accounts for the full endorsement given by the land grant association at the same time that NUEA gave only qualified support. The proposed labor extension bill gives land grant colleges specific recognition during the initiatory phase of the labor extension service. It says:

---

41. *Proceedings of the Thirty-Third Annual Meeting of the National University Extension Association at the Hotel Shoreland, Chicago, Illinois, May 2–5, 1948* (Bloomington, Indiana: Feltus Printing Company, Inc., 1943), pp. 196–97.

"Cooperating institution" means any college, school, or institution in any State receiving the benefits of the Act of July 2, 1862, and August 30, 1890, and Acts supplemental thereto, and any other public or private nonprofit college, university, or research agency in any State, certified as eligible by the State board.[42]

This section of the bill can be interpreted to mean that the original state board will be composed of six representatives of the land grant college and six of organized labor. Since this board passes on the qualifications of other institutions of higher learning applying for recognition, the position of the land grant college is excellent.

This section of the bill may also explain why Keller's institution, a land grant college, sent Professor Anthony Luchek, head of its Labor Education Service, to Washington on February 20, 1948, to testify affirmatively in behalf of Penn State before the same committee before which Keller had appeared.[43]

In line with Keller's testimony, however, the NUEA, after heated debate, tabled a resolution endorsing the labor extension bill at its annual business meeting on May 5, 1948.[44] At its 1949 meeting, the NUEA stated that it is in favor of the "principle of federal aid to workers' education provided it is administered through institutions under public control."[45] Yet key members of NUEA admit that probably both this workers' education bill and a general adult education bill eventually will be passed.[46]

A broad analogy may be drawn between NUEA and AFL attitudes on the labor extension service bill. Fortunately, NUEA opposition is based upon specific application of the act; it does not undermine the act's entire structure as does the AFL position, but it does show a lack of necessary flexibility.

Anyone who is at all familiar with legislative maneuvering, particularly in Washington, knows that no bill can be too specifically

42. *Senate Bill No. 110, op. cit.*, p. 14.
43. *Labor Education Extension Service*, Senate Document no. 72321, Eightieth Congress, Second Session (Washington: U.S. Government Printing Office, 1948), pp. 256–58.
44. *Proceedings of the Thirty-Third Annual Meeting of the National University Extension Association, op. cit.*, p. 172.
45. *Proceedings of the Thirty-Fourth Annual Meeting of the National University Extension Association, op. cit.*, p. 134.
46. Charles A. Fisher, Knute O. Broady and Cyril O. Houle, *Adult Education in the Modern University* (Ann Arbor, Michigan: University of Michigan Press, 1949), p. 39.

drawn when it is introduced, and that all bills undergo changes in subcommittee, in committee, and on the floor. The NUEA Committee on Government Information and Action is aware of this fact. It must also be aware that, because education has historically been a function of the state government, it is unlikely that Congress will pass and appropriate funds for a federal aid bill which does not function through a state agency, in this case either a state university or a land grant college. It is almost certain that the labor extension service bill finally passed will be very similar to agricultural extension service legislation and very close to what Keller has said the NUEA wants.

However, just as the AFL may prefer no bill at all to one which routes funds and services through institutions of higher learning, the NUEA may prefer no bill at all to one which appropriates specifically for workers' education instead of generally for adult education. If these prove to be their attitudes, both organizations will be guilty of holding back progress and of keeping unionists from getting the training they both need and want.

2

Problems Facing College and University Workers' Education

HEAVIER STATE APPROPRIAtions and enactment of even limited federal labor extension service legislation will help workers' education hurdle the obstacle of finance. But more money will not resolve present differences within and between organized labor and colleges and universities regarding the role the latter should play in the workers' education movement. Neither will additional funds help solve other than financial problems facing institutions of higher learning now operating workers' education programs.

As yet, no statement as to the proper function of the current programs has won general acceptance from both organized labor and higher education. As a result, both the programs and their directors lack full status.

The disagreement as to the role that institutions of higher learning should play exists within those institutions, within the labor movement, and between universities and the labor movement.

At one extreme are people and groups who assert that colleges and universities do not belong in the field of workers' education. At the other extreme people and groups insist that institutions of higher learning should carry on the major share of workers' education activity. In between are those who see the function of institutions of higher learning as supplementary and complementary to the programs conducted directly by and within the labor movement.

This diversity of outlook is due in part to the fact that the American labor movement is neither fully accepted nor considered fully established by the whole community. Some colleges and universities fear the reaction of other powerful groups in the community to educational services conducted for union groups. Some labor leaders are afraid that relatively new union members are not sophisticated enough to be exposed to college teachers many of whom, they fear, are neither sympathetic to nor experienced in labor.

Another basic reason for disagreement on the role of colleges and universities in workers' education may be found in the fact that the present public is the product of a social heritage of agrarian individualism. Much of that public still looks upon workers' education as class education and, therefore, abhorrent as part of the American way of life. Workers, one often hears, are part of the American community and should be educated through the general adult education facilities available to all citizens.

A third basic reason for confusion is the division within the labor movement itself as to the role colleges and universities should play in workers' education.[1] It is obviously impossible to define the university's function in the field of workers' education if professional educators in the labor movement itself cannot agree on what they think it should be.

Perhaps the major reason for this confusion is the belief held by labor generally that management exercises the controlling voice in the affairs of institutions of higher learning. Unions are unwilling to accede to management's assumption of the right to guardianship over the policy and function of educational services for workers such as those provided from 1944 through 1948 by the Workers Educational Service of the University of Michigan. They have serious reservations regarding the establishment of college and university

1. George Guernsey, *op. cit.*, p. 6.

workers' education programs within industrial relations and labor-management institutes, particularly where such institutes are supervised by schools of commerce and colleges of business administration whose primary responsibility is service to business and industry.

Labor also feels that university student bodies and faculties, by and large, are drawn from the upper and middle classes. Bankers and businessmen predominate on university boards of trustees. Because universities are subject to control by middle and upper class groups, labor is of the opinion that, at worst, universities are trying to undermine the labor movement and that, at best, they do not understand the needs and problems of workers and are likely to be patronizing in their attitudes toward the labor movement.

Fact justifies labor's concern about the control of our colleges and universities. The direct influence of organized labor in shaping the "selection and study of social and economic problems is feeble by comparison with that of opposing pressure groups."[2] It is no secret that the strongest influences on university boards of trustees come from vested interests generally opposed to the kind of social and economic reform that is most beneficial to the wage earning sections of the population.

Hubert P. Beck's study of thirty leading American universities discloses that in 1934–1935, only 3 out of a total of 734 trustees could be said to represent the views of organized labor.[3]

This poor showing, particularly where public institutions are concerned, is partly attributable to labor itself. In only rare instances have labor leaders, through city and state labor bodies, appointed education committees to study the constituency of boards of control in their areas, and only in rare instances have they taken the lead in helping select and elect liberal candidates for such boards of control.

Agreement between unions and institutions of higher learning suffers also from labor's proclivity to apply generally a grievance it has against a specific university or against a specific individual within a university. While it is true that some professors have not yet discovered the existence of the labor union, or at least have not inte-

2. Baker, *op. cit.*, pp. 255–56.
3. Hubert P. Beck, *Men Who Control Our Universities* (New York: King's Crown Press, 1947), p. 59.

grated it into their theories, this attitude is not universal. As Marius Hansome says:

> First, it is the height of infantile folly to condemn indiscriminately all of the departments of a university be it state-endowed or privately financed, merely because its political science or history division harbors some illiberal defenders of the status quo. Second, if the organized work-people aspire toward the social direction of public affairs, they will need science and technique as handmaidens, and therefore, an uncritical opposition toward the extension of university instruction to the work-people would, in the terminology of the Russian Communists (who ought to know from their experience with the post-revolutionary exodus of the "intellectuals") be considered "counter-revolutionary," or in plain English, damned foolishness.[4]

Nevertheless, it is just such uncritical disapproval which forms the basis of AFL's opposition to the labor extension service legislation now before Congress. And the events leading to the termination of the Workers Educational Service of the University of Michigan, in turn, are responsible for the jaundiced view the AFL now takes of college and university workers' education.

What happened in Michigan points up the problem raised when management claims stewardship over college and university educational activity designed specifically for workers.

Strangely enough, the attack on the Michigan program began in Washington, D.C., not in Detroit where the WES office was located, a fact which buttresses the belief that those responsible were attacking workers' education in general as well as the Michigan program in particular.

Testifying before a House Labor and Education subcommittee which in May, 1948, was holding hearings on the labor extension bill, Adam K. Stricker, Jr., an economist for the General Motors Corporation, charged that a part-time lecturer for WES was teaching the "Marxist idea of class economics" in a course, two sessions of which he had attended. The lecturer was Sam Jacobs, educational specialist for the UAW–CIO who had been a teacher in the Detroit public schools, a lecturer at Wayne University, and an OPA official in Wash-

4. Marius Hansome, *World Workers' Educational Movements: Their Social Significance* (New York: Columbia University Press, 1931), p. 502.

ington. President Alexander G. Ruthven of the University of Michigan immediately refuted Stricker's statement, saying, "Everything that someone doesn't like seems to be construed as Marxism." He defended Jacobs' course as one "which is designed to stimulate thinking on a controversial issue rather than one in which all material presented is to be accepted as factual."[5]

Stricker complained that two UAW labor economics pamphlets were passed around in the class, one of which stated that whenever GM president C. E. Wilson thought of labor his mind always went back "to his $30,000 bull (if he could only stick a ring in each worker's nose) . . ."[6] WES director Arthur A. Elder admitted that Jacobs "may have made a mistake" in using these pamphlets, but established the fact that Jacobs' course was based upon the President's Economic Report for 1948.[7]

What initially appeared to be illustrative testimony supporting a particular position regarding national legislation soon became fuel for flames arising around a controversial project of the University of Michigan Extension Division. The editorial pages of the Detroit dailies took up the cudgels. On May 21, 1948, both *The Detroit News* and *The Detroit Free Press* commented on WES. Said the former:

> The essential mistake was not, as the director of the extension service now thinks, the teacher's for distributing the pamphlets, but the University's, *for retaining the spokesman of a private interest to provide public instruction at the public expense.*[8]

According to the latter:

> . . . classes given by the U. of M. extension service should be, first and last, objective. Yet that is palpably impossible if the instructor, as in Jacobs' case, is to be a professional propagandist for a particular cause.[9]

While these papers showed unanimity in concluding that an employee of the labor movement was, by virtue of that employment, disqualified as a university instructor, neither paper condemned the University of Michigan for its principle of hiring men regularly em-

5. *The Detroit Free Press*, May 20, 1948.
6. *The Wage Earner*, May 21, 1948.
7. *The Detroit Free Press*, May 20, 1948.
8. *The Detroit News*, May 21, 1948.
9. *The Detroit Free Press*, May 21, 1948.

ployed in the fields about which they teach. For example, when in the same year of 1948 the University of Michigan established a program in real estate education and appointed one Charles Sill, then a member of the Real Estate Board, as coordinator, neither paper took cognizance of his appointment. The university regularly employs experts in other fields to teach out of their rich background of training and experience. In fact, unless university extension everywhere followed this practice, its programs would be dead affairs.

Stricker's charges were made to look even more ridiculous when three supervisory employees of the Michigan Bell Telephone Company who had been attending Jacobs' class stated of their own volition that they "saw nothing subversive, and heard nothing aimed at changing either the American government or present economic system" during the sessions.[10]

Nevertheless, Michigan's Governor Kim Sigler, on June 10, summoned University of Michigan officials to the state capitol for discussions, and before the end of the month WES was suspended.

On October 16, the Board of Regents of the University placed the WES program under the direct supervision of E. J. Soop, director of university extension, and on October 19, Arthur A. Elder was told that his position as coordinator was to be abolished because of this change in WES administration.

Indignation at these decisions was widespread. Labor organizations throughout the country, newspaper columnists, prominent churchmen, educators and other community leaders protested vigorously. One such protest written by W. K. Kelsey, author of the Commentator column in *The Detroit News*, is especially worth quoting:

> It was announced Wednesday that the University of Michigan School of Business Administration will offer undergraduate training for careers in Chamber of Commerce work.
>
> This is the same University of Michigan whose Board of Regents recently dismissed Arthur Elder, director of its workers' educational service — a service suspended after a General Motors employe had criticized the teaching of a single course.
>
> A brief investigation has brought information that undergraduate training for careers in Board of Commerce work was requested by the State organization of Chambers of Commerce, representing about 100 of them. The informant, an

10. *The Detroit Times*, May 21, 1948.

Problems Facing University Programs

official of one of these organizations, also remarked that so far as he knew, all the Chambers of Commerce in Michigan were completely staffed, and that he believed there were not 300 vacancies in the entire country.

If this information is correct, it would seem that the University's School of Business Administration will offer training which, however valuable, has little chance of application for the purpose toward which it is directed. On the other hand, several thousand students of the so-called working classes were enrolled in the courses which the Regents have seen fit to suspend — it may be for now and it may be forever.

The Commentator asks again the questions which still remain unanswered: For whom and by whom is the University of Michigan being run? For the business interests, or for the people? By the business interests, or by the people?[11]

Because others were asking the same questions put by Kelsey, the Michigan Committee on Civil Rights established a Commission of Inquiry on the Workers Educational Service. Members of the commission were Professor John L. Childs of Columbia University, adult educator Winifred Fisher also of New York City, attorney John Ligtenberg and William R. Ming of Chicago, and William A. Crane of Toledo.

After two days of hearings, March 19 and 20, 1949, the commission reached the following conclusions:

> 1. A promising state experiment in workers education began in 1944 under the auspices of the University of Michigan: promising in its fundamental educational principles, in the groups that united to plan and carry it out, and in the results achieved during the four years it was in operation.
>
> 2. This program was interrupted under ambiguous circumstances which, because of the opposition to the program which had been expressed by certain business and political forces, led inevitably to the conclusion that this opposition was responsible for the University's action. Unfortunately the Board of Regents and the President of the University acted so secretly as to support rather than to dispel this idea.
>
> 3. The program which the University offered to substitute for the original is not well conceived. It marks a definite re-

11. *The Detroit News*, October 28, 1948.

treat from the original plan for workers education. It does not command the confidence of the people and organizations it was designed to serve, and it involves the loss of a staff which had been successful in serving those people and organizations. If persisted in, this substitute program will not only set back workers education in Michigan but in the rest of the nation.

4. This case is not primarily one involving civil rights; rather it raises issues of the integrity of educational institutions and programs, and of the values and purposes in workers education.[12]

The substitute program to which the commission referred was set up in October, 1948, as part of general extension. This program was a university effort on behalf of workers rather than a partnership with workers as was WES. It was set up without consultation with the duly appointed representatives of the public, the Michigan faculty, and organized labor who had advised WES. It was not surprising, therefore, that when the substitute program offered a group of seven classes in January, 1949, only two students came forward to register. Of course, the program was discontinued.

Since that time, the University of Michigan has had no active program in workers' education and has no program of its own in prospect.

The commission, finally, called upon Michigan's then new Governor Mennen G. Williams to re-establish an "educational program for workers through partnership between organized education, labor and the public." It made this recommendation because, in its opinion, "the modern state in the United States cannot afford to leave any large segment of the population out of its educational plan."[13] There have been recent indications in Michigan that some kind of workers' education program will be established and will be administered through the State Department of Public Instruction rather than by the state university.

The fate of the Michigan program is an object lesson to both the labor movement and institutions of higher learning. It points up the destructive potential of direct management interference in an area where management is well advised when it is asked to forego

---

12. *Report and Recommendation, Commission of Inquiry on the Workers Educational Service of University of Michigan* (Detroit: Michigan Committee on Civil Rights, 1949), pp. 5–6.
13. *Ibid.*, p. 10.

even representation on advisory boards to agencies solely concerned with workers' education. Edwin Witte makes this point succinctly:

> But I believe it to be a grave mistake for management to insist upon representation on governing or even advisory boards concerned with workers' education. University workers' education is an educational service for unions and union members. For management to insist that it be accorded a voice in the control of this type of adult education will expose it to the charge that it seeks to control the unions and their activities. . . . it is no more appropriate that management should have a voice in the control of workers' education than that labor should share in the control of institutes and classes for foremen, personnel managers, and business executives. No one who has demanded that management be given a place on the governing or advisory boards concerned with workers' education has yet raised his voice to place labor on boards concerned with management education and no university has put labor on such boards.[14]

Phillips Bradley, out of his experience as director of both Cornell University and the University of Illinois labor-management institutes, asserts that management which opposes workers' education is putting itself in an untenable and dangerous position. He says that a shift of balance of power in society which this kind of attempted suppression may induce, could result, in turn, in attempts on the part of labor to suppress management education.[15]

Management which either condones or desires to emulate the actions of General Motors in Michigan is unable to bring itself to accept the fact that workers' education must ask probing and disturbing questions if it is to make a contribution to our evolving democracy. Most colleges and universities have supporters of both liberal and conservative points of view on their staffs. The strength of institutions of higher learning, like the strength of the American nation, lies in diversity of groups and diversity of opinion. As long as every group may be heard and every opinion stated, neither higher education nor the nation is in danger.

14. Witte, *op. cit.*, pp. 21–22.
15. Phillips Bradley, "The University's Role in Workers' Education," *Adult Education Journal*, 8:83, April, 1949.

Fortunately, from his research Paul Essert can predict that progressive management will come more and more to recognize organized labor as "an accepted institution of our economy" and will "welcome a more educated leadership" in the trade union movement.[16]

Closely related to the problem of the stewardship of college and university workers' education are problems which come out of higher education's relative inexperience in the field and its wariness in launching programs of workers' education.

Survey and experience demonstrate that too many colleges and universities tend to set up administrative and curricular programs of workers' education on traditional educational patterns in higher education. They ignore the principles of modern adult education and plan as if they are launching formal undergraduate and graduate curricula.

Many programs of this type, as well as some of those more realistically organized, are placed under the general supervision of schools of business administration and commerce whose traditional and primary function and outlook is to serve business and industry. Labor asserts that where this procedure is followed, it indicates failure to recognize that unions are important in their own right and are entitled to service in terms of their own interests and problems.

Over half the college and university workers' education programs surveyed consider their primary function to be direct immediate involvement in attempted improvement of industrial relations. They emphasize the need for labor's appreciation of management's problems. Labor says that there should be equal emphasis on the need for management's appreciation of labor's problems and that consideration of the immediate and internal problems of unions is prerequisite to this exchange and should be the first concern of college and university workers' education.

The continued existence of problems such as this has led a small group of leaders and workers' education specialists within the labor movement to carry their condemnation of college and university workers' education to the extreme. They present another problem.

These people say that workers' education must be financed solely on workers' money and controlled and managed solely by workers' organizations. They say that workers' education can no more be out-

---

16. Essert, *op. cit.*, p. 10.

side the labor movement than can trade unions themselves. These people are the isolationists of the workers' education movement.

Some educators consider these extremists to be in the throes of adolescence. T. R. Adam says:

> An exaggerated sense of independence from the rest of society tends to convince them that all possible objectives may be obtained from the development of their own resources. In the educational field this leads to the mirage of an independent system of continued learning conducted by workers for workers. The cost and burden of educational instruments created by the community over a long period of years is dismissed as irrelevant by dreamers of a self-sufficient proletariat. The complete capture by organized labor of public education is toyed with by other political un-realists. The practical objective of using established institutions of learning to provide the ordinary wage earner with a fairer share of educational opportunities attracts little attention from the enflamed champions of the abstract worker.[17]

Other authorities see this attitude as symptomatic of growing pains within the labor movement. Dr. Mollie Ray Carroll points out that both school and job have tended to spell compulsion to the average worker. Particularly young workers and members of newly established unions look upon labor organizations as a weapon for imposing their will on others as society has imposed its will on them. "Given time and spared crushing defeat," she says, "they come to see unionism as a constructive and cooperative force and to induce employers and others to share their view."[18]

College and university inexperience and hesitancy in developing programs of workers' education is largely responsible not only for this extremist clique, but also for the major problem which institutions with programs face today. Survey and experience show that few institutions of higher learning make the necessary distinction between workers' education and labor-management education.

Workers' education can be defined as that education which endeavors to make the worker a better person, a more effective member of his union group and a participating citizen in his community. It

---

17. Adam, *op. cit.*, p. 149.
18. Mollie Ray Carroll, "The Emergency Education Program and Labor," *Journal of Adult Education*, 6:494, October, 1934.

is designed to enable workers to understand their own experiences and problems, out-plant as well as in-plant.

Labor-management education endeavors to promote understanding of the problems that arise out of the employment contact. Workers explore some of the problems facing management and vice versa. Workers' education is broader and more inclusive in content than labor-management education, even though it restricts itself to workers' problems.

Perhaps the best way to point up the difference between the two is to contrast the operating statements of two institutions, one of which, in 1947, conducted a workers' education program and the other of which still carries on a labor-management education program.

Arthur A. Elder listed the general objectives of Michigan's WES as follows:

> 1. To help participants in the program to become better members of their workers' groups.
> 2. To assist participants to become more intelligent and effective citizens in the community.
> 3. To assist local unions and workers' groups in developing democratic leaders in the locals and in the community.
> 4. To interpret and work for improved understanding of the program and the objectives of organized labor by other community groups.
> 5. To help organized labor to develop a better understanding of its responsibility, in the community and in the nation.[19]

Lynn A. Emerson, in 1947 acting director of the New York State School of Industrial and Labor Relations at Cornell University, stated his program's policy as follows:

> It is necessary that understanding of industrial and labor relations be advanced; that more effective cooperation among employers and employees and more general recognition of their mutual rights, obligations, and duties under the laws pertaining to industrial and labor relations in New York state be achieved; that means for greater responsibility on the part of both employers and employees be developed; and that industrial efficiency through the analysis of problems relating to employment be improved.[20]

19. *Proceedings of the Thirty-Second Annual Meeting of the National University Extension Association, op. cit.,* p. 72.
20. *Ibid.,* p. 69.

Problems Facing University Programs

To cite this difference is not to say that WES did not concern itself with the employment contact and deal with management problems in some of its activities. It is not to say that Cornell does not concern itself with workers' education activities. The point is that the *primary* emphasis in each of the programs as first stated was different.

Labor is not opposed to labor-management education. For the present, labor asks that universities *emphasize* workers' education. Actually, it is to labor's interest that businessmen and professionals should learn something of the aspirations and problems of labor through joint educational activities, and labor can benefit through further educational contact with management aspirations and problems.

Unions state that joint programs should be conducted only where the parties make mutual requests and where there is real purpose in staging such programs. Far too many institutions of higher education conduct them as "window dressing."

Caution in arranging joint programs is particularly necessary now that the National University Extension Association has expanded its workers' education committee into an industrial relations and workers' education committee. Correspondence and conversations indicate that member institutions will more readily enter the expanded area because labor-management education is not so controversial as is workers' education. Yet, if they attempt to conduct programs without adequate surveys of local labor-management relationships and without consulting both sides of the bargaining table, institutions of higher learning will only further antagonize the labor movement.

The AFL has taken cognizance of the implications in this situation and has issued the following statement to its affiliates:

> Recently there has been an inclination on the part of some state federations to invite representatives of management to participate in planning and conducting these labor institutes and thus transforming them into labor-management institutes. Some universities have established schools of industrial and labor relations and are particularly interested in cooperating with such joint institutes. If your group is interested in such a joint project, we shall be glad to advise you concerning it.[21]

21. John D. Connors, *How to Set Up a Labor Institute* (New York: Workers Education Bureau of America, 1947), p. 5.

One valuable by-product of the expansion of labor-management education has been more widespread recognition of the potential of workers' education. Often, where educators have started out with the sole objective of organizing joint classes and other activities in labor-management relations, they have come to the conclusion that there is a prior and complementary job to be done within both managerial circles and the labor movement. Accordingly, they have begun to develop separate classes, discussions, conferences and institutes for both labor and management groups. On the basis of experience with these programs, some institutions of higher learning have found later joint activities well received by both parties.

Jesuit schools of industrial relations, particularly, have done a great deal of joint work with labor and management. A director of one of these schools has found, somewhat to his surprise, that joint activities are very well received. Perhaps part of the reason, in his case, is that he did conduct workers' education activities prior to the establishment of his joint program.[22]

As prominent an authority as Eduard Lindeman sees a future trend toward more joint undertakings. He attributes past timidity of colleges and universities and past suspicions of union people to ideological involvements which, in his opinion, are now disappearing. He contends that both labor and management are becoming more aware of their responsibilities for making American democracy work and concludes that the "overwhelming responsibility which rests upon both should lead to rapid movement in the direction of joint undertakings."[23]

A survey conducted by the author indicates that Lindeman is unjustifiably optimistic when he talks about rapid change in the direction of joint labor-management undertakings. Be that as it may, workers' education is not as suspect as it once was and the change, in part at least, is due to contact with workers' education conducted by the new labor-management institutes lately established at such staid universities as Cornell, Rutgers, Illinois and California.

There is growing awareness that workers have been neglected as a group by universities while the specialized educational needs of other segments of the community have been well served. In addition, of

22. Leo Cyril Brown, "Catholic-Sponsored Labor-Management Education," *Journal of Educational Sociology*, 30:512, April, 1947.
23. Quoted in Alfred P. Fernbach, *University Extension and Workers' Education* (Studies in University Extension Education, No. 3. Bloomington, Indiana: The National University Extension Association, 1945), pp. 4–5.

Problems Facing University Programs

course, many colleges and universities are seeing that if they are to continue their growth or even to save themselves from losing ground, they must widen the basis of their popular support.

As a matter of pure selfish interest, institutions of higher learning must win the support of organized workers in order to keep their proper share of an increasingly haggled-over tax dollar. Unless universities show by their actions that they are seriously attempting to serve labor in terms of workers' needs and interests, their efforts will prove abortive and they will find labor returning to its old suspicions regarding institutions of higher learning. The difference will be that those suspicions will be intensified.

Harsh words have been said in professional circles regarding neglect of workers' education. In 1940, B. C. Riley of the University of Florida, then president of the National University Extension Association, reported that only five members of NUEA were conducting institutes in cooperation with the Workers Education Bureau of America. He charged that universities were not fulfilling their obligations to labor and asked his colleagues to do something about the situation.[24]

Riley's charge was not without a basis in fact. NUEA always has given verbal support to workers' education; very few of its member institutions have implemented policy with campus action.

Where action has been taken, misunderstandings often have arisen. Washington University's Frank Debatin points out that educators far too frequently fail to inspire confidence when they conduct negotiations with labor.[25] George B. Zehmer, Director of Extension at the University of Virginia, asserts that educators do not take due account of the necessity for giving unions "something to say about what is being done for and to them."[26]

Typical of the far too common reaction to labor's requests for educational services is an excerpt complete with underscored words from a letter written by a member of the faculty of a large midwestern state university:

> This university, so far as I know, does not discriminate with respect to workers or others. . . . Whether a person is a

---
24. *Proceedings of the Twenty-Fifth Annual Convention of the National University Extension Association, op. cit.,* p. 94.
25. Frank Debatin, *Administration of Adult Education* (New York: American Book Company, 1938), pp. 437–38.
26. Quoted in Creese, *op. cit.,* p. 74.

"worker" or from the ranks of management or a profession has *no bearing* on his eligibility. Such requirements as exist are professional or technical and not *class* requirement.

Another correspondent, this time from the faculty of a well known West coast school, said with evident discouragement:

> A workers' education program is not being conducted by our school. We have made sporadic attempts to have some single classes in conjunction with unions, but haven't had much luck. I guess we haven't an administration willing to back such a program.

But the overt antagonism to workers' education observable in these two letters is no more unfavorable than total ignorance as to what workers' education is all about. One large mid-western state college passed along an inquiry to its Supervisor of Employment who replied as follows:

> ———— at the present time does not have an organized program of education for its workers. There has been some talk of starting such a program with some of our employee groups but as yet nothing has been organized. At present, we do not have any organized labor groups on the Campus and of course, the demand for such an educational program has not been pressing from the standpoint of the employers.

Attitudes such as these help one understand labor's suspicions of university people and its reluctance to cooperate fully with them without prior consultation on aims and objectives.

Labor knows that the Morrill Act offered each state a generous land grant as endowment for a college devoted chiefly to teaching agriculture *and the mechanic arts*. Yet, extension services which have evolved out of broad interpretation of the act and through extension of the act in subsequent legislation have been applied largely to the farm group.

Labor is concerned, too, that universities have made little use of the experience in workers' education that has been accumulating since 1921. Some colleges and universities are completely unaware of that experience, but many which are aware of it apparently do not see its relevance to the newer programs that have been mushrooming since 1944. These universities have entered the field of workers' edu-

Problems Facing University Programs 43

cation with faculties and administrations most of whose members have had little or no contact with labor. These people have no real aptitude in dealing with the worker in the classroom, and no real experience with or knowledge of the teaching methods which have been found effective in workers' education.

Part of the responsibility for this situation and for general neglect of workers' education on the part of colleges and universities must be given to the labor movement. To cite an example, the Workers Education Bureau for years has been left to negotiate with universities in the name of labor with almost no power to apply the militant social pressure necessary to make its claims effective. The AFL has stinted the Bureau both in terms of financial support and in terms of backing for its policy and program. Similar inadequate support can be cited from CIO experience.

In addition to these larger problems, the solution of which requires top level policy decisions from both the labor movement and institutions of higher learning, there are practical operational problems encountered every day which need attention.

While final answers for many of these operational difficulties are inextricably linked to resolution of broader policy issues, college and university programs now functioning cannot work in a vacuum. They must meet their day-to-day needs as best they can.

Many programs have lay and faculty advisory committees. Program directors are at least partly responsible for determining the functions of members of these committees. Those programs surveyed unanimously report that they are under-financed and under-staffed. Program directors must make decisions relative to the types of service they will offer, the instructors and discussion leaders they will use, and the materials they will utilize in providing the educational services they offer. They must arrange for consultation and for the cooperative development and evaluation of their program with the labor groups they are asked to serve; they must also provide for maintenance of liaison with such groups once service has begun.

3

Organization and Administration of College and University Workers' Education

ALTHOUGH COLLEGES AND universities now conducting workers' education programs face many vexing problems, they are establishing a remarkably good record of sound achievement.

The following survey is based upon inquiries sent to eighty-three institutions believed to have workers' education programs. Twelve reported that such work had been discontinued. Of the remaining seventy-one, thirty-five answered a lengthy questionnaire;[1] eighteen provided usable information in other forms and eighteen merely indicated that they conducted workers' education activities. Fourteen of the fifty-three institutions on which information was obtained were, in addition, observed at first hand.[2]

Of the fifty-three institutions studied, twenty-eight are public and twenty-five are private. Of the public institutions, fourteen are state

1. See Appendix I.
2. See Appendix II.

Organization and Administration

universities, five are land-grant colleges, seven are both state universities and land-grant colleges, one is a state college and one is a municipal university.

Twelve of the private institutions are non-sectarian and thirteen are under religious control — in every case Roman Catholic. It is interesting to note that eleven of the latter were established by the Society of Jesus. The preponderance of Jesuit activity in the field indicates the extent to which that order has made a policy of the establishment of industrial relations institutes as part of its Institute of Social Order.

Geographically, in every section of the United States, except the South and Southwest where little or nothing in the field is now being done at the university level, either public or private institutions of higher learning are carrying on programs of workers' education.

Size of institution, strangely enough, has little relevance so far as the extent and coverage of the workers' education program is concerned. Goddard College in Vermont, for example, carries on activity broader in scope than that existing at many larger institutions.

Appendix II indicates that there is wide variation in titles of the various agencies within institutions charged with the workers' education function. Title has little importance as an indicator of whether or not a given institution carries on workers' education. Divisions of adult education, schools of education, labor-management institutes, colleges of business administration, departments of economics, and even a library are some of the parts of colleges and universities which have assumed responsibility for workers' education at their institutions.

Titles of persons in charge of such programs vary as greatly as the labels given the university divisions operating in the field. In most cases, these persons have professorial rank. In some cases they have dual titles such as professor of economics and head of labor education service. In other cases, these people hold dual appointments such as half-time in liberal arts and half-time in university extension.

There is also great variance in supervision of workers' education programs. Of thirty-three program heads and two assistant program heads reporting, thirty-four designate the university officer or agency to whom they are responsible. These designations in order of frequency of mention are:

Supervisor	Institutions
President	16
Dean of Extension	7
Director, Institute of Industrial Relations	3
Dean, College of Arts and Sciences	2
Chancellor	1
Dean of Administration	1
Economics Department Chairman	1
President through Provost	1
Three man committee	1
Not clearly defined	1
	34

In almost every instance, accounting is made to a regularly recognized administrative officer of the university. The fact that most workers' education program administrators report to the higher echelons of university administration is an indication of the present touchiness of their position within the university family. College and university administrators apparently wish to keep a ready eye on their "problem children."

Another indication of the delicate position of directors of workers' education is to be found in the fact that, while all of them are of professorial or equivalent rank, an uncommonly large proportion of them lack tenure. Of thirty-two directors questioned on this point, only sixteen reply in the affirmative. Public institutions report ten directors with tenure, Roman Catholic colleges and universities have six, and non-sectarian institutions claim one.

No one can claim that this situation results from doubt concerning the qualifications of those directors. Without exception they have impressive and extensive training and experience in their chosen field. Sixteen of them present background in government, twenty have experience in the labor movement, ten have worked in management, and all thirty-five, of course, have university experience. Most of them have university background other than in workers' education — a preponderance are economists.

Twenty-five directors list their major background in the university field, four have had most of their experience in the labor movement, three come out of government, and three out of management circles.

It is quite natural, in view of the long-standing ties between certain institutions and individual professors within institutions and labor organizations, that most of the current crop of workers' education directors in colleges and universities should come from within the universities themselves. However, the supply of qualified university personnel is limited and it is a matter of concern to labor leaders that only four of the present directors have predominantly labor backgrounds while three of them are ex-management men.

Yet, most directors are influenced by lay advisory committees on which labor is fully represented. While it is both desirable and sensible to appoint qualified people from within the labor movement as administrators of university workers' education programs, it is doubtful that labor can claim that many of the present directors are not suited to their positions. Those directors who may not have as much labor experience as unions deem necessary, can and do learn much from labor members of lay advisory committees.

Twenty-three institutions report that they have lay advisory committees. One state university reports that it selects a lay labor advisory committee for each major project it schedules, but that it does not maintain a regular committee.

These lay advisory committees range in size from two to thirty-five members and break down as follows:

Number on committee	*Number of institutions*
35	1
20	2
19	1
15	1
12	2
9	2
8	3
7	3
6	1
5	1
4	5
2	1
	23

The institution with the largest committee selects all members of that committee from the labor movement.

Of two hundred thirty-two people now serving on lay advisory committees, ten come from government, one hundred forty-six from labor, forty-seven from management and twenty-nine may be classified as public. The labor movement should be encouraged by the fact that so high a proportion of advisors to workers' education agencies within colleges and universities come directly out of trade unions.

Nine state, six religious, and two non-sectarian institutions report that their lay advisory committees are appointed. Four religious institutions, all Jesuit, indicate that theirs are elected.

As is the case with workers' education program directors in institutions of higher learning, members of lay advisory committees, for the most part, are selected by the top university administration. The large number of committees selected by the workers' education director are all in Jesuit institutions where that procedure apparently is the established practice. It is encouraging to note, however, that as many committees are picked by union groups as are selected by university presidents. The breakdown on lay advisory committee selection is as follows: in four instances the committee is chosen by presidents of institutions, in four by union groups, in two by boards of trustees of institutions, in one by a faculty committee, and in eight by the workers' education program director.

The length of the terms for which lay advisory committee members are appointed varies as much as do selecting agencies. Five institutions put members on indefinite tenure, one sets a term of six years, two set three-year terms, four set one year, and one state university selects committee members for the length of specific projects.

Each of the four Jesuit institutions which has an elected advisory committee permits its worker students to do the balloting. In every case, committee members hold office for one year.

Many lay advisory committees, nine to be exact, meet for quarterly discussions, four meet semiannually, two meet annually, and seven do not meet at stated intervals but come together on call. All four elected committees have regularly scheduled meeting dates.

Functions of these lay advisory committees differ in detail but can be placed under two broad headings. Fifteen institutions report that their committees give general advice. Only two indicate that their committees help with the planning and promotion of specific activities. And one state university reports that the committee it chooses

Organization and Administration 49

for each project it undertakes is a real working committee. Typical replies illustrate what these lay advisory committees do.

Professor Anthony Luchek, head of the Labor Education Service at Pennsylvania State College, says that his advisory committee is made up of thirty-five members selected by state-wide labor organizations — AFL, CIO, and Independent. The committee meets for one day each year to discuss a prepared agenda which it may change or enlarge. The major function of this meeting is to review past programs and to recommend future direction. It is Luchek's opinion that the committee functions helpfully because each member is briefed before the meeting on what has happened and on the problems the program faces. Committee members add to the content of Luchek's program by making definite suggestions about the needs of labor organizations.

The Institute of Labor and Industrial Relations at the University of Illinois, reports Director Ellison Chalmers, has an advisory committee of five labor, five management, and five public representatives. This committee meets once or twice a year to discuss the general direction of the program.

Assistant Director Vidkunn Ulriksson of the School for Workers at the University of Wisconsin states that his program has a nine-man advisory committee: four from the AFL, four from the CIO, and one from the International Association of Machinists. The purpose of this committee is to advise and help the staff in a general way. The committee has three scheduled meetings a year and is on call for other meetings.

Probably the committee with the most specific function is that which advises the University of Chicago Union Leadership Training Project. According to Director A. A. Liveright, the committee, made up of ten CIO members, eight AFL members, three Independent unionists, and a sprinkling of labor lawyers and professors from other institutions, helps frame the program and gives it real guidance. Committee members recruit for the program, with over half the committee participating directly.

Workers' education program directors are unanimous in their opinion that informal day-to-day relationships with individual members of lay advisory committees are equal to or more valuable than formal committee meetings. This opinion has special significance for directors of workers' education programs which operate within the framework of labor-management institutes. Since lay advisory committee members concerned with such institutes are from management and public agencies as well as from labor, and must necessarily be concerned with the entire scope of the body they advise when they meet, it is essential that workers' education specialists working within labor-management institutes feel that they can confer informally at any time with lay labor advisors on the problems and needs of labor groups and on the efficacy of the content and methods they are using to help solve those problems and meet those needs.

Not a single workers' education program administrator who has a lay advisory committee states that that committee is of no value to him. On the contrary, every administrator testifies to its practical importance.

Complementing these lay advisory committees in sixteen colleges and universities are faculty advisory committees. Seven state universities, six religious and three non-sectarian institutions utilize faculty committees.

Faculty advisory committees generally are smaller than lay advisory committees. The largest has thirteen members, and the four smallest have three each.

Of the eighty-nine faculty members currently serving on these advisory committees, the largest number, thirty-six, come from colleges of liberal arts. Seventeen are on business administration faculties, fourteen in extension work, two each in education, engineering and industrial relations, eight are on graduate faculties, four come from law faculties, three from schools of speech, and one from a workers' education program.

In eleven instances, members of these committees are chosen by college and university presidents; in four, again the Jesuit schools, by the workers' education program director; and in one by the dean of extension.

Five faculty advisory committees which meet regularly do so on a quarterly basis, one meets monthly, one semiannually, and one annually. Eight of the sixteen faculty advisory committees now functioning meet only on call.

As might be expected, functions of faculty advisory committees in most cases are more specific and greater in variety than those of lay advisory committees. While eight institutions indicate that their faculty advisory committees are charged with giving general advice,

Organization and Administration

each reports concrete examples of what this charge amounts to in assistance to the program. In practice what they do is not at all unlike what is done by faculty advisory committees in other fields. Three other committees are asked to help with educational materials and outlines, members of four others are drawn into planning and evaluating sessions with unions, and one committee actually is the final authority on all matters relating to the operation of the program.

Most of the original course outlines, study guides, discussion sheets and other educational materials used at Rutgers were either the work of or were checked by members of the faculty advisory committee.

At Roosevelt College, Chicago, according to Labor Education Division Director Frank McCallister, four liberal arts men and one business administration man join on call with two faculty members from McCallister's division to check thoroughly what has been done to help project what should be done.

Cornell has a unique committee composed of the entire faculty of the New York State School of Industrial and Labor Relations. The committee meets periodically to discuss and advise upon reports of extension activity with labor groups. In addition, says Director of Extension Ralph Campbell, individual members of that faculty are consulted regularly for advice concerning aspects of the extension program in the areas of their specialization. Further, many members of this faculty teach and lecture on the extension program and help develop teaching materials and extension bulletins.

Father George Lucy, Labor-Management School Director at the University of San Francisco, states that his faculty advisory committee of four members — two from liberal arts and two from business administration — in addition to giving the usual consultation and advice on course outlines and course materials, helps secure instructors and speakers for the program.

Like lay advisory committees, faculty advisory committees for workers' education programs within colleges and universities are very useful. Not a single institution which has one indicates, with the exception of the usual dissatisfaction with certain individuals on committees, anything but praise for the assistance given the program by faculty advisory committees.

One of the problems with which lay advisory committees can and do assist is the key problem of finance. Particularly in the case of public institutions where the university proposes and the state legislature disposes, influential labor and other community leaders who are members of such committees can go directly to the governor, other top state administrators, or the members of the legislature with statements of what workers' education programs do, what they propose to do, and of what their necessary costs are and are likely to be. Lay advisory committees in private institutions can assist those colleges and universities when they make appeals to the varied sources from which they usually derive a large portion of their revenue exclusive of tuition and fees.

Despite assistance from lay advisory committees, the financial resources of every current college and university workers' education program are inadequate to the demand for service.

Only three institutions report that state funds are specifically earmarked for their workers' education programs. One of them got $12,000 for the year 1950–1951, one received $35,000 for the same period, and the third institution failed to report the amount appropriated.

Sixteen colleges and universities indicate that they receive grants from their own general budgets to carry on workers' education. In the seven instances where a definite figure was given for the fiscal year 1950–1951, the largest amount quoted was $26,000 and the smallest was $650. Six institutions indicate that their yearly appropriation from the administration, considered without exception to be too low, varies considerably.

Fees are collected by fifteen institutions. But neither fees nor the amount per year they bring in can be structured into a meaningful pattern. One university collected $40,000 in fees in one year — it is the exception. The four other institutions reporting listed amounts from $6,000 to $400. Five colleges and universities indicate that the total amount of fees collected varies from year to year.

Not a single institution charges a fee for consulting with a labor group on its educational problems. Fees are charged by most institutions for three kinds of educational activities: classes, discussions or lectures, and conferences or institutes.

Colleges and universities collect two types of class fees. Where individuals register for short term classes, a set fee per person is charged; where classes are scheduled for specific union groups, a set group fee is charged. Some institutions indicate that they utilize both individual and group fee systems.

Organization and Administration

Although the fee per person ranges from $1 to $15, in most cases it is set at $5 or less. The fourteen institutions reporting individual fees break down as follows:

Amount of fee	Number of institutions
$ 15	2
9	1
6.50	1
5	4
3 to 5	2
3	1
2.50	1
2	1
1	1
	14

It is worth noting that Jesuit colleges and universities, with one exception, do not charge fees. However, they do solicit contributions ranging from $2 to $5 from all who are willing to pay. The Harvard Trade Union program has a tuition fee of $400 and the Chicago Union Officers Program asks $165 tuition for credit and $75 without credit.

The largest group fee requested is $200 per class and the smallest is $20 to $25.

Six institutions indicate that they charge for lecture, film and filmstrip discussions. Individual fees are either one dollar or fifty cents. The highest group fee is $30 and the lowest from $5 to $25, depending upon the size of the group.

The greatest range of fees is found in connection with conferences and institutes. The reason for this lies in the fact that there are many different types of activity which can be listed under the conference-institute heading. Twelve colleges and universities reported fees required as follows:

Amount of fee	Number of institutions
$ 1 to $60	2
12 to 15	1
1 to 12	2
10	2

1 to	6	1
	5	2
	2	1
	1	1
		12

Meals and lodging for conferences and institutes in all cases are on a cost basis, with rates varying according to the area in which the college is located. Dormitory accommodations range from $1 to $2.50 per night. Breakfasts are priced from forty to seventy-five cents, lunches from fifty cents to $1.25, and dinners from fifty cents to $1.75.

Two institutions quote a weekly (six days) rate on lodging and meals; one asks from $30 to $35, the other $25. A third institution sets a rate of $2.25 per day to cover both items.

It should be evident from the incomplete character of these figures that colleges and universities in workers' education are reluctant to give out information on appropriations and fees. Many of them, although indicating that they receive funds from the university and fees from students, hesitate at becoming specific. They usually claim that the figures vary too much to be useful, or that the information is not readily available.

Figures on cost per activity are even more difficult to gather, partially because the administrators of the programs are overworked and understaffed and cannot give the matter proper attention. This is doubly regrettable because it will be almost impossible to obtain the money needed for workers' education programs unless the authorities who control appropriations can be given an accurate picture of costs.

Here and there, colleges and universities have attempted to estimate cost per activity and to ascertain what proportion of cost comes from appropriation and what proportion from fees. One institution reports that the cost of an average class is $120, with $80 coming from appropriation and $40 from fees. Another institution says that an average class costs $75, with half coming from appropriation and half from fees.

Information on the cost of discussions is equally hard to obtain. In two out of three reported instances, half of the required amount comes from appropriation and half from fees. In the other case, two-thirds of the cost is taken from appropriation and one-third is received in fees.

Most conferences and institutes are run on a cost basis, with fees set just high enough to cover salaries and expenses for instructors, lecturers and speakers.

While exact figures on costs are difficult to elicit, generally, program administrators attempt to get as much as possible of the cost of programs from either legislative or university appropriations and to keep fees at a minimum. However, there is also general agreement on the advisability of charging some kind of fee for services rendered, on the basis that people seldom appreciate that which costs them nothing.

To define the function of workers' education programs is as vitally important a problem as finance. While it is obvious that no program can be sustained without adequate funds, it is not equally obvious to many colleges and universities that funds are of no real value unless the program which they finance has objectives that commend themselves to the people whom that program is designed to reach.

Something already has been said about the current confusion regarding the proper role of colleges and universities in workers' education. In an attempt to dispel some of that confusion, each college or university working directly with labor groups was asked to indicate which of three statements submitted best explains the function its workers' education program is considered to perform.

Two of these statements are philosophical in character; the other is quite functional. The distinction between the philosophical and the functional was laid down for a very good reason. Many workers' education specialists firmly believe that an empirical and pragmatic approach to the field is the only sensible one. Instead of a philosophy, they prefer a statement of a few basic specifics on content, technique and approach.

One philosophical statement, which combines the thought of J. B. S. Hardman and Ernest Schwarztrauber, is oriented toward satisfaction first of labor's immediate and internal needs.[3]

3. J. B. S. Hardman, "The Challenge and the Opportunity," *Fifth Yearbook of the John Dewey Society* (New York: Harper and Brothers Publishers, 1941), pp. 7-8; and E. E. Schwarztrauber, *"The Wisconsin Idea" in Workers' Education* (Madison, Wisconsin: University of Wisconsin School for Workers, 1946), p. 7.

The function of the university in the present status of industrial relations is to give organized labor educational facilities whereby it can satisfy those internal needs that will help build it to some degree of equality with industry. This means that the university should aim at equipping the worker with tools that will enable him to become a better wage-earner and a better union member.

The "understanding" and the "learning to know one another" that is expected between labor and management will then arise not in class room contacts but around the conference table in contract negotiations. And there, too, will take place the ironing out of conflicting interests.

The other philosophical statement, which combines the stated policy of the Cornell program with what has been said by the University of Virginia's A. P. Fernbach, is oriented toward immediate, direct involvement in the improvement of industrial relations.[4]

The underlying assumption of a program of workers' education is that such specialized training will contribute to better industrial relations. Representatives of both labor and management should be brought together by the university in a common training program for mutual and cooperative analysis of the problems common to both groups. Such a common approach to these problems will bring greater understanding and appreciation of differing attitudes and will serve to narrow the areas in which conflicts of interest or disputes may arise in the future.

The functional statement is provided by Professor Anthony Luchek of Pennsylvania State College.[5] It asserts that workers' education:

1. Is *adult* education for *workers* on a *voluntary*, non-credit basis.
2. Uses *informal* teaching techniques.
3. Provides workers with a better understanding of their status, problems, rights and responsibilities as *workers, as union members, as consumers* and *as citizens*. (Will broaden their conceptual horizons, teach certain skills

---

4. *Proceedings of the Thirty-Second Annual Meeting of the National University Extension Association, op. cit.,* p. 69; and Fernbach, *op. cit.,* p. 7.
5. Anthony Luchek, "Workers' Education in Three Universities" (unpublished paper, The Pennsylvania State College, State College, Pennsylvania, 1949), p. 2.

Organization and Administration

  and/or train in the use of certain information.)
 4. *Will lead to group action in solving* the above.

Of the forty-one colleges and universities selecting one of the three statements, twenty-one pick the philosophical definition oriented toward immediate direct involvement in improvement of industrial relations. Thirteen select the functional definition. Only seven colleges and universities choose the definition oriented toward satisfaction first of labor's immediate and internal needs.

Nineteen institutions of higher education state that they have a written policy concerning the function of their workers' education program; five say that they have an understood but not a written policy; and sixteen indicate that they have neither a written nor an understood policy.

The following statements of policy are typical of institutions which orient their service to labor toward improvement of industrial relations.

The Institute of Industrial Relations at St. Joseph's College, Philadelphia, has an objective which it calls broad but not vague:

> Employer and employee are natural partners, charged to reach a joint solution of common problems. And their cooperative effort, as all acknowledge, must grow from mutual understanding and mutual respect. But this worthy goal is impossible unless both are guided by a fundamental philosophy of right and obligation, honesty and fair play, a keen determination to rule out degrading selfishness, an equally keen insistence that business and profit, work and wages must be geared to the happiness of people.[6]

At the University of Bridgeport, the Institute for Labor and Industrial Relations says that it is organized to "promote industrial understanding in Greater Bridgeport by offering lecture discussion courses in subjects of current interest."[7]

The Institute of Labor and Industrial Relations at the University of Illinois is directed to "foster, establish, and correlate resident instruction, research and extension work in labor relations."[8]

---

6. *Courses of Instruction in Labor-Management Relations 1950–1951* (Philadelphia: St. Joseph's College Institute of Industrial Relations, 1950), pp. 5–6.
7. *Institute for Labor and Industrial Relations* (Bridgeport, Connecticut: University of Bridgeport, 1950), p. 2.
8. *Extension Services in Labor and Industrial Relations* (Champaign, Illinois: Institute of Labor and Industrial Relations, University of Illinois, 1950), p. 2.

Illustrative of workers' education programs which orient their efforts toward satisfaction first of labor's immediate and internal needs are the following statements.

Rutgers, the State University of New Jersey, in describing the work of its Institute of Management and Labor Relations, proceeds on the premise that:

> . . . organized labor *does* want stable industrial relations, but that these come best through first satisfying the primary and immediate internal needs of workers — needs which often seem to have no apparent direct bearing on labor-management relations but which, in the long run, affect them most profoundly.
>
> This means that the Rutgers Institute Labor Program, generally, helps workers to understand their own needs and problems before it expects them to appreciate the problems of management; and that it keeps its activities as broad and as functional as appropriations and legislatively prescribed scope permit.[9]

Chicago's Roosevelt College calls its Labor Education Division an integral and expanding part of that college.

> The Division's purpose is to provide labor leaders and members with the knowledge and skills necessary to understand and evaluate their organizations and themselves and to function more effectively in their union positions. It emphasizes not only collective bargaining techniques and methods of union administration, but also studies of labor history and of social, economic and political trends affecting workers as members of the labor movement and as citizens.[10]

The Workers Education Program of Rhode Island State College says:

> The purpose of the Workers Education Program is to provide educational opportunity for industrial employees. It is designed to afford a more complete knowledge of current labor principles and practices, as well as instruction in occupational

---

9. Irvine L. H. Kerrison, "Rutgers Serves New Jersey Labor," *Workers Education Bureau News Letter*, 12:7, June, 1950.

10. *Training for Better Union Service* (Chicago: Labor Education Division, Roosevelt College, 1950), p. 3.

Organization and Administration 59

subjects and matters of general interest to workers as intelligent citizens of a democratic society.[11]

All five of the colleges and universities which indicate that their definitions of function are understood but not written, state that their over-all objective is to train leaders who will contribute to better industrial relations.

Statistics and statements of function, at first glance, seem to substantiate the oft-repeated charge of the labor extremists that colleges and universities are not as much interested in workers' education as they are in labor-management education. A thorough examination of the facts, in most instances, dispels this notion. The difficulty is that most colleges and universities do not bother to spell out their objectives and services. If one were to take literally the stated Illinois function, he would conclude that fostering, establishing and correlating extension work in labor relations spells out a narrow and highly specialized operation. In practice, such is not at all the case. Classes, discussions and conferences conducted by Illinois in cooperation with union groups have a wide scope. The Illinois Institute of Labor and Industrial Relations conducts an annual journalism workshop for labor editors and, in 1950–1951, it developed a series of regional conferences on labor and public relations.

In fact, in a good many cases, labor-management institutes established at colleges and universities during the last decade, either have begun or are considering beginning a broadening of their function of service to labor in terms of its felt needs and problems.

State legislatures which have established, and institutions of higher learning which currently are conducting, workers' education programs have chosen to place most such programs within labor-management institutes, thus assuring the literal-minded of equal attention to labor and management. Labor leaders can challenge the reasons for this policy, but they cannot legitimately charge that merely because an agency is titled "Labor-Management Institute," it cannot have a bona fide workers' education program.

Twenty institutions either commit themselves directly to programs oriented toward labor's internal problems and needs or to a functional approach that leads automatically to the same commit-

11. *Workers Education Program* (Providence, Rhode Island: Division of General College Extension, Rhode Island State College, 1950), p. 2.

ment. Of the twenty-one remaining colleges and universities which define their function in workers' education, a substantial number either have begun or are beginning to broaden their function in the direction that commends itself to labor.

That the labor movement generally approves the work of most of these institutions is attested to in "testimonials" from union groups. Conventions of both national and state labor bodies have passed resolutions commending college and university workers' education and requesting more funds for it. Unions have provided scholarships for extension class programs and on-campus summer schools. Labor leaders have called upon legislative representatives and government administrators to promote plans for expanding college and university workers' education programs. Rank and file unionists have sent colleges and universities letters of appreciation for what they are doing.

Twenty-seven colleges and universities report that labor organizations in their areas have passed convention and meeting resolutions and have made statements supporting the workers' education programs conducted by them. Only eleven institutions state that they have never been publicly praised by the labor movement.

The Convention Education Committee of the AFL commended the Harvard Trade Union Program to that body's 1949 convention and called for establishment of similar resident programs at other universities.[12]

At the same convention, Delegate Lewis M. Herrmann of the Typographical Union referred to the work of the Rutgers Institute of Management and Labor Relations and urged delegates from other unions and other states to promote similar programs at their state universities.[13] The California State Federation of Labor in 1950 passed a resolution commending the work of the University of California in workers' education.[14]

These are not isolated instances of consideration given by formal conventions to college and university workers' education programs. Year in and year out, at convention after convention both national and state, committee reports of this kind are made and resolutions of this kind are passed and reported back to the colleges and uni-

12. *Labor and Education in 1949, op. cit.,* p. 30.
13. *Ibid.,* pp. 30–31.
14. Letter from Ronald W. Haughton, August 4, 1950.

Organization and Administration 61

versities conducting workers' education activities. But commendation of this nature is not merely a matter of routine business to be handled at convention time. When the Michigan fiasco broke, the AFL and CIO, as well as many international unions and statewide labor bodies, took immediate action condemning what was happening to a program vital to the educational needs and interests of the labor movement.

College and university workers' education program directors can report all kinds of "testimonials." And in every instance where resolutions have been passed and commendations given, there is a functional relationship between college and university programs and labor officials in the area responsible for workers' education activity. University programs are considered complementary to what the union is doing in the field. Certain activities are best handled within the labor movement; certain other activities can be handled just as well or better by college and university workers' education. Reasons for this belief should become clear as we examine the types of services offered by workers' education programs in institutions of higher learning.

4

College and University Workers' Education Programs Today

COLLEGES AND UNIVERSIties are offering ever broadening programs of workers' education to union groups. In practice, they are extending themselves far beyond the specific stipulations of purpose contained in the legislative acts and institutional directives that have created most of them.

Research is one function of these programs which is just beginning to develop in scope. George Counts and Theodore Brameld point up the need for closer cooperation between scholars and union research departments. They suggest joint committees for the dissemination of economic, political and social data assembled by both.[1]

Most labor-management institutes established at colleges and universities since 1944 conduct research into industrial relations problems. But research conducted by those institutes specifically for labor

---

1. George S. Counts and Theodore Brameld, "Relations with Public Education; Some Specific Issues and Proposals," *Fifth Yearbook of the John Dewey Society* (New York: Harper and Brothers Publishers, 1941), p. 268.

groups on problems of their own choosing has been almost nonexistent.

Only four colleges and universities report that their departments responsible for workers' or labor-management education do specific research work for the labor movement. The University of Minnesota, one of the institutions which does conduct such research, states that it will accept grants for cooperative research in conjunction with union organizations provided that such research holds promise of making significant additions to the knowledge of the field under investigation, and provided that the university maintains full control of and responsibility for studies initiated.[2]

Union groups are asking that more colleges and universities make their facilities available for specific labor research studies. There exists today not a single union research department adequately financed or staffed to study its own problems, those of the industry in which the union functions, and those of the economy in general.

Unions appreciate, and universities today provide, reference services which enable the former to better conduct what research they are able to carry on. Labor-management institutes offer reference services including pertinent books, professional journals, technical and specialized reporting services like the Bureau of National Affairs loose leaf reports, company and union newspapers, periodicals and pamphlets, psychological testing materials, and information about audio-visual aids.

Twelve union and university people, all of whom are directly engaged in workers' education and all of whom are consultants to the Union Leadership Training Project of the University of Chicago, have banded together to work out an exchange service on workers' education materials. Lists of these materials are prepared periodically at the Institute of Labor and Industrial Relations at the University of Illinois and are available to interested individuals. The cooperating agencies are listed in Appendix III. These materials are extremely useful to colleges and universities which conduct or contemplate conducting workers' education programs.

But, by and large, research and aids to research geared to union needs and problems and available through institutions of higher learning still are inadequate to the demand.

2. *Program of the Industrial Relations Center* (Minneapolis, Minnesota: University of Minnesota, 1950), p. 12.

It is in offering extension classes to workers that colleges and universities, again still far from adequate to the demand, make their broadest contribution to workers' education. Forty-seven institutions report that they conduct such classes.

Most of the institutions conducting classes provide both on and off-campus instruction — only nine, mostly Jesuit, restrict their activities to the campus. Fifteen institutions hold classes in union halls, ten use extension centers, twelve use public school buildings, and nine use parochial schools. YMCA, YWCA, YMHA facilities, hotels, libraries, clubs, settlement houses and radio stations are used to a lesser extent. The variety of facilities utilized underscores the functional nature of class activity — the carrying of services to the people.

The majority of classes conducted are of the short term variety, although in a few cases classes run the equivalent of a full academic semester or longer. A breakdown on the number of sessions per course conducted follows:

Number of sessions per course	Number of institutions
36	1
33	1
24	1
20	1
8 to 16	1
15	1
6 to 12	5
10	2
8 to 10	3
6 or 8	4
4 to 8	1
5	1
2	1
Varies	4
	27

There is more uniformity in the frequency of sessions per week per course than in the number of sessions per course. Of the twenty-seven institutions reporting, twenty-five state that classes are held once

University Programs Today

each week, one says that classes are conducted twice per week, and one states that it holds classes three times per week.

At nineteen institutions class sessions are two hours long, at four they are one hour long, and at four others forty-five minutes.

Many colleges and universities claiming to conduct some kind of workers' education activity naturally report that they hold classes for workers only. Seventeen institutions are in this category. Eight institutions report that they conduct classes for labor and management together, fifteen have classes for labor, management and the public together, and seven conduct separate classes for management and public groups as well as for labor groups. Several colleges and universities conduct more than one of these different types of classes.

It is worth repeating at this point that the decision to run separate classes for workers, or some kind of joint participation classes, should be governed by the individual situation.

But whatever the decision made, because most institutions currently operate their programs within labor-management institutes, attention should be given to the advice of Phillips Bradley to the effect that integration of services to management and labor is important at two levels within the university structure: there must be consultation on both over-all program and specific projects between the people responsible for labor and management programs, and both programs should operate through university extension.[3] Unless the former exists, division of services along the lines of clientele could result in conflicting community group pressures, with changes in balance of power between labor and management creating constant turmoil in the academic divisions paralleling these groups. Unless the latter is observed, liaison between the campus and the community serviced will suffer.

These comments on integration apply to discussion forum, conference and institute and all other services, in addition to extension classes, provided for labor groups.

During the academic year 1949–1950, colleges and universities conducted 668 extension classes for labor groups. Three institutions scheduled over eighty classes each. Another institution conducted as few as two classes. The breakdown on workers' education exten-

3. Bradley, *op. cit.*, p. 87.

sion classes conducted by the twenty-two colleges and universities reporting is as follows:

Number of classes	Number of institutions
88	1
87	1
80	1
60	1
39	1
36	1
34	2
32	1
30	1
28	1
19	1
18	1
16	3
12	1
9	1
5	1
4	1
3	1
2	1
	22

It is obvious that, despite the upsurge of college and university workers' education since 1944, the majority of institutions in the field have been conducting less than forty extension classes per year, for the record shows that their activities are increasing year by year. Supply and demand certainly are not in balance. There could be no more potent argument for the immediate establishment of a national federally-financed labor extension service.

A total of 13,226 workers enrolled in classes during 1949–1950. One institution, that which conducted eighty-eight classes, served fifteen hundred people. At the other extreme, fifty-one persons were aided by the institution which conducted only two classes. The majority of the colleges and universities reporting served between three hundred and six hundred workers each.

Reports on activities from college and university workers' education programs, as well as brochures and announcements, emphasize

University Programs Today

that, despite the relative weakness of the over-all effort, a wide variety of subject matter is available to labor groups. This variety indicates that attempts are being made both to meet workers' actual and concrete needs as trade unionists and to develop a widening interest which may eventually involve the workers' consideration of every aspect of world economic, social and political life. The large number of institutions offering the so-called "bread and butter" subjects indicates, too, that colleges and universities, in many instances, are beginning where labor's dominant interests and needs now are.

Titles of courses currently offered can be grouped in six categories: internal trade union, industrial relations, labor-community relations, general skills and techniques, management organization, and function and moral emphasis.

Courses which have an internal trade union emphasis are those specifically designed to assist the worker to develop satisfactions for his own needs and solutions for his own problems as a member of an increasingly important organized group within the community. Seventeen such courses are now being offered by university workers' education programs.

They break down as follows:

Title of course	No. of institutions offering course
Accounting for Unions	3
Basic Trade Unionism	12
How to Organize	1
Labor Economics	28
Labor History	46
Labor Journalism	6
Labor Problems	38
Labor and Public Relations	5
The Office Employee	1
Political Action for Unions	3
Seniority Principles and Problems	1
Steward Training	26
Trade Union Methods	1
Union Administration	8
Union Counseling	4
Union Leadership Training	5
Workers' Education Techniques	5

Most institutions are interested in offering courses which are likely to be non-controversial. While forty-six offer labor history and twenty-eight give labor economics, only three offer political action for unions and only one offers a course on how to organize. However, aside from the fact that the latter two titles are much more controversial than the first two, there is much to be said for the point of view that courses in organizing methods and political action properly belong in the sphere of union education departments. They are highly specialized and must be geared to a given organization or a given program to be really effective.

It is encouraging to find so large a number of institutions offering labor problems and steward training and to see at least a few colleges and universities concerning themselves with subjects like union counseling and labor and public relations.

As might be expected, more institutions offer courses in the industrial relations category than in any other. These are the courses concerned with the bargainable or controversial issues facing both labor and management. Upon successful resolution of the problems raised under these course titles depends the future welfare of our economy. When colleges and universities approach these topics with the objective of getting more information to the parties who have to bargain across the table, the courses will be extremely valuable. When and where institutions of higher learning consider that the mere teaching of these subjects automatically will bring industrial peace and eventually perhaps the elimination of the bargaining table, the courses are at best naive, and at worst, dangerous. Course titles and the number of institutions now offering them follow:

Title of course	No. of institutions offering course
Arbitration	7
Collective Bargaining	47
Guaranteed Annual Wage	1
Health, Welfare and Pension Plans	16
Industry-wide Bargaining	1
Job Evaluation	17
Labor Legislation	44
Negotiations and Grievances	19
Profit Sharing	1

Railway Labor Legislation	3
Safety	3
Taft-Hartley Law Breakdown	4
Time and Motion Study	27
Wage Incentives	3

Of these fourteen courses it is not at all surprising that collective bargaining is the only one given by every institution offering extension classes to labor groups. Labor legislation, without doubt because of labor's preoccupation with the Taft-Hartley law, is only a shade less popular as a class subject. Skill subjects, like time study and job evaluation, are receiving more and more attention from college and university workers' education programs. Increasing attention also is being given to the fringe benefits course — that on health, welfare and pension plans.

Courses with a broader community basis also are becoming popular. Colleges and universities currently are offering nine courses which fit into the labor-community category. These are the courses which emphasize concepts and functions which apply to unorganized as well as to organized American workers and to workers in other countries as well as to American workers. The very fact that some of these courses are demanded and supported by labor groups underscores labor's desire to promote community integration. Statistics on these courses follow:

Title of course	No. of institutions offering course
Community Relations	10
Cooperatives and Credit Unions	3
International Labor Relations	2
Labor and Government	10
Social Security	9
Unemployment Compensation	6
Wages, Prices, Profits	2
Workmen's Compensation	6
World Affairs	2

Labor and government courses differ from political action courses in that they are broader and take in the evolution and current status of the entire labor-government relationship. Workmen's and unemployment compensation courses do not compete with social security courses because the latter deal almost wholly with old age and survivors' benefits and because much time is spent, in the former, on routine and claims. At whichever of these courses we look, however, we must conclude that it embraces some of the problems or needs of all workers and that it is evidence of labor's concern for the total community as well as for itself.

Courses giving instruction in general skills and techniques, a fourth category, are not forgotten in workers' education at the university level. Some of these courses offer training in newer or advanced skills; others are concerned with what, in workers' education as elsewhere, are called basic or core subjects. Seven courses currently fall into this general skills and techniques category:

Title of course	No. of institutions offering course
Conference and Group Leadership	4
Economics	16
English	6
Human Relations	21
Public Speaking and Parliamentary Procedure	43
Radio Workshop	2
Visual Materials Workshop	1

The large number of courses offered in public speaking and parliamentary procedure and in human relations is evidence of labor's continuing concern with training in the rudiments of leadership. Courses in group leadership, and radio and visual materials workshops illustrate labor's alertness to the desirability of keeping up with relatively new techniques being successfully utilized by other community groups.

One interesting ramification of the English course is a current concern of the Rutgers program. A large garment union with a heavy concentration of foreign-speaking membership in a central New Jersey city has asked the Rutgers Institute of Management and Labor Relations to conduct classes which combine English with the tenets of democracy and basic trade unionism. This is an opportunity to perform a functional educational service which cannot be done through the regular public school Americanization program. It is illustrative of the potential for broadness which lies in college and university workers' education.

Also illustrative of this broad potential is the fact that two institutions of higher learning offer workers a course in Industrial Organization and Management, one offers a course in Production Management and Control, and six offer a general survey course labeled Industrial Relations Procedures Today. These are the few courses in the fifth category of management organization and function. For the mature and sophisticated union leader such courses can be highly useful.

A sixth category, that entitled moral emphasis, covers some of the courses offered only by Roman Catholic colleges and universities, and breaks down as follows:

Title of course	*No. of institutions offering course*
Catholic Faith in Practice	4
Communist Tactics	3
Ethics	11
Labor's Rights and Responsibilities	8
Logic	4
Rights and Duties of Management and Labor	6

No other organized religious group has entered the workers' education and labor-management education fields to an extent even approaching that fostered by the Roman Catholic Church and particularly the Society of Jesus.

Today over twenty-five labor schools affiliated with the Jesuit Institute of Social Order are part of a common program enunciated by the Vatican and operated through the hierarchy of the Society of Jesus. The basic principles of the program are contained in the Papal Encyclicals on the Social Order. The major objective of the program is to promote more harmonious labor-management relations by educating both labor and management to their moral obligations and by instilling in each party respect for the rights of the other.

This Roman Catholic interest in workers' and labor-management education, while it dates back to the first decade of this century, got its real impetus after 1940. In addition to the more than twenty college and university programs conducted by the church, over sixty parishes or dioceses conduct labor schools or forms of one kind or another.[4]

The university, parish and diocesan labor and labor-management schools are serviced but not sponsored by the Social Action Department of the Roman Catholic Church in America. This department also conducts, through its Institute on Industry, a summer school for working girls and, through its auxiliary Catholic Conference on Industrial Problems, several two-day meetings annually on the relation of Roman Catholic teaching to current economic and social problems.[5]

Through these media, the Roman Catholic Church is able to inform its members of church teachings regarding the role of labor unions and the role of industrial relations in our economy.

While Jesuit as well as public and non-sectarian colleges and universities do more with extension classes than any other medium for transmitting workers' education, a sizable group of institutions (20) conduct lecture and film discussions for workers on either a "spot" single or series basis.

As is true with classes, discussions are held both on and off the campus. Fifteen institutions restrict this activity to the campus; seventeen conduct discussions either off the campus or both on and off the campus. Those utilizing off-campus facilities use a wide variety of them. Discussions are held in union halls by fifteen colleges and universities, in extension centers by six, and in public schools by eight. Discussion groups also meet in parochial schools, parish halls, libraries, YMCA's, hotels, clubs, bars, and at conferences and conventions held by various labor organizations.

Seventeen colleges and universities report that they conduct discussions for workers only; twelve hold them for labor, management and the public meeting together; and four hold separate discussions for labor, management and public groups.

In 1949–1950, colleges and universities conducted 915 lecture and film discussions which were open to workers and with which their workers' education agencies were directly involved. One institution

---

4. Brown, *op. cit.*, p. 510.
5. Frederick G. Hochwalt, "Catholic Adult Educational Activity," *Handbook of Adult Education in the United States*, Mary L. Ely, Editor (New York: Institute of Adult Education, 1948), p. 189.

accounted for 600 of these discussions. Another was responsible for only one of them. The breakdown on the seventeen institutions reporting is as follows:

Number of discussions	Number of institutions
600	1
77	1
40	2
28	1
20	3
15	1
10	2
9	1
8	1
7	1
6	1
4	1
1	1
	17

These figures demonstrate that discussions are less extensive than are extension classes. Without the one institution with so disproportionate a share of them, the showing would be poor indeed.

A total of 24,775 workers were served through college and university workers' education discussions during the academic year 1949–1950. One institution was in contact with over 10,000 people through this medium; another institution reached only 50 people. The majority of the institutions reporting indicated that they served between 500 and 1500 workers through film and lecture discussions. While fewer discussions than extension classes were held, a much larger number of people was reached through the discussions. In addition, generally, a different type of worker was reached.

Classes are conducted primarily for union functionaries of one kind or another; discussions usually are held for rank and file union members at regular union membership meetings.

Discussion topics are more varied than are extension class course titles. Typical of the approach of colleges and universities in this area is the following quotation:

> The Institute provides discussion outlines, sound films or stripfilms, complete audio-visual equipment, and a competent

leader for topics in which your group is interested and for as much time as your group wants to give.[6]

There are three major reasons why discussion programs are not offered more frequently: unions give priority to skill and technique training for stewards and officers; a good many colleges and universities lack audio-visual equipment and personnel; and there is not as yet a wide selection of films and filmstrips available on topics in which union people are interested. On this latter point it should be stated that many current films and filmstrips that do not deal directly with the usual workers' education topics are adapted through preparation of discussion outlines which point up their omissions and which supplement their deficiencies.[7]

Most union groups prefer film discussions to straight lecture discussions, because, for obvious reasons, they feel that the former will hold the interest of the members to a greater degree.

One who is familiar with the film "Union at Work" produced by the Textile Workers Union–CIO, and the film "This is the SIU" produced by the Seafarers' International Union–AFL, or with the filmstrip "Saga of 666" produced by the United Automobile Workers–CIO and the filmstrip "Labor's Challenge" produced by the American Federation of Teachers–AFL, knows that the stories told and the skills and techniques imparted have a good chance of reaching the audience because an appeal is made to both eye and ear.

This same thing can be said of the film "Steelworker Comes to the Campus" produced by Pennsylvania State College, and the filmstrips "Public Relations for Labor" produced by the University of Illinois, and "Unemployment Compensation: What Do You Know About Your Law?" produced by Rutgers, the State University of New Jersey.

Films and filmstrips are useful at on- and off-campus conferences and institutes, as well as for membership meeting discussions.

Off-campus institutes and conferences constitute the fourth category of extension service offered by college and university workers' education programs. While most institutions in the field conduct such meetings on-campus throughout the year, colleges and universities are now beginning to expand their service to include re-

---

6. *Your State University Provides: An Answer to Labor's Educational Needs,* *op. cit.,* p. 7.
7. Irvine L. H. Kerrison, "Using Films and Stripfilms with Union Groups," *Film Forum Review,* 3:14, Winter, 1948–1949.

gional off-campus institutes and conferences. At present, twelve institutions report that they do so. Eight institutions say that they hold conferences at union halls, seven use extension centers, eight use public schools, while religious buildings, libraries, hotels, clubs and other facilities are used to a lesser extent.

Seven colleges and universities hold off-campus conferences and institutes for workers only, two conduct them for labor and management together, five schedule them for labor, management and the public together, and five institutions conduct separate programs for labor, management and public groups.

During the 1949–1950 academic year, one institution scheduled twenty-five off-campus conferences and institutes, and another offered twenty-four. Six other institutions offered a total of twenty-nine off-campus programs, bringing the total for the year to seventy-eight.

These seventy-eight off-campus conferences and institutes were attended by 9,894 people, with one institution serving over four thousand and another reaching as few as ninety-four persons. Most of the institutions reporting indicated that they served between three hundred and six hundred people each.

Off-campus institutes and conferences are conducted on a variety of subjects, but the objective in many instances is to help union groups with immediate and internal problems.

During the winter and spring of the academic year 1949–1950, the Rutgers Institute of Management and Labor Relations conducted in the major New Jersey cities a series of "Labor and the Community" conferences designed to help labor learn techniques for cooperating with community organizations of all types. Five such conferences, bridging the state from north to south, were held. In each instance, plans were laid and speakers and discussion leaders selected by a joint committee on which both the university and key union groups in each area were represented. Although dates for the conferences, time schedules, and other details varied from place to place, there was surprising similarity in the decision as to what the conferences should cover. Actually, one over-all pattern was used, embracing the topics: Why Community Relations? Structure and Organization of *Our* Community; How Labor Fits into *Our* Community; Developing Working Relationships with Other Community Groups.

These conferences proved to be extremely helpful in orienting diverse labor groups to their communities and in assisting them to begin the learning of skills and techniques necessary for the development of functional relationships with other community groups.

In every case, the conferences have been followed by additional classes. Several central labor unions and industrial union councils are now conducting, in cooperation with Rutgers, labor-community and labor-public relations classes for specially selected committee members who are working with other community groups. Students are perfecting the techniques they began to appreciate at the community-wide "Labor and the Community" conferences.

Off-campus institutes and conferences are being conducted both on rather broad topics and on topics as specific as time study, grievance handling and union counseling. In many instances, programs of the latter type substitute for extension classes, particularly where union membership is scattered over a wide geographic area and regularly scheduled weekly extension classes are not likely to be well attended. In addition, programs of this type can be utilized to bring all segments of the labor movement together in a particular area for a day or two of study on problems common to them all. The university can be the catalytic agent in areas where organizational differences between labor groups make it difficult for one of those groups to take the initiative.

Closely related to the conference and institute program is the on-campus summer school program conducted by fifteen colleges and universities.

The best known and most extensive of these summer schools for workers is that at the University of Wisconsin, which has had over a quarter-century of experience in the field. The activities of the Wisconsin school are fully described in the voluminous writings of Ernest E. Schwarztrauber, one of the most influential minds in the history of the American workers' education movement.

Some colleges and universities, among them Ohio State, Indiana, and Goddard College in Vermont, place emphasis upon on-campus summer work with labor groups. One union, the United Steelworkers of America–CIO, to date at least, similarly has stressed on-campus summer activity in its workers' education program.

Of the fifteen colleges and universities currently scheduling summer schools, eleven hold them for workers only, three conduct them for labor, management and the public together, and one holds separate schools for labor and management groups.

During the summer of 1949, twelve institutions held a total of fifty-four schools in which labor participated. One institution conducted eighteen such schools and three held as few as one each. The breakdown on summer schools for workers that summer is as follows:

Number of summer schools	Number of institutions
18	1
7	1
6	1
5	1
3	5
1	3
	12

A total of 2,795 persons were served through these summer schools, with one institution serving as many as 1,100 and another serving as few as 15 people.

Most of these summer schools serve a double purpose — they provide education and they offer recreation. They are a combination of classes such as those conducted throughout the year on an extension basis: speeches and discussions given or led by "visiting firemen," and indoor and outdoor recreation. Unions are now encouraging their key members to spend summer vacations at such schools so that they can have both recreation and an opportunity to improve themselves as active union members and as participating citizens in the community.

Typical content and schedule of a summer school for workers is illustrated in Appendix IV.

Perhaps the greatest physical barrier to the development of more short-term resident conferences, institutes and summer schools is the present inability of most colleges and universities to duplicate the Continuation Center at the University of Minnesota which was built in 1936 at a cost of three hundred thousand dollars, 45 per cent of which came from the Federal Works Project. Colleges and universities seldom have dormitory space available during periods when full-time students are in attendance; groups coming to the campus, therefore, must either plan to stay for one day only or arrange to lodge in hotels or other commercial facilities, a process which not only is expensive but one which also, because it separates people, tends to break down rapport established through meetings on the campus.

At Minnesota, the Continuation Center has year-round residence accommodations for eighty people — lounge, library, dining halls, conference and classrooms — reserved for the use of all kinds of groups which wish to come to study at short-term residence conferences and institutes.

The need for more facilities of this kind is emphasized when we add the number of workers served through on-campus summer schools to the numbers served through classes, discussions and off-campus conferences and institutes during the academic year 1949–1950. A grand total of approximately 50,690 workers participated in college and university-conducted workers' education that year. Facilities like those at Minnesota undoubtedly would have done much to increase this number had they existed at other institutions of higher learning.

The short-term resident institutes made possible by facilities of the continuation center type offer a distinct advantage, particularly for the highly specialized and more advanced workers' education with which colleges and universities more and more will be concerned. They permit concentrated intensive study, which is the next best thing to long-term on-campus resident study. Yet opportunities today for conducting such institutes during the academic school year are exceedingly scarce, as is full-time resident instruction for workers. The Harvard Trade Union Program, cut from nine to three months study, is the only thing being done which can be considered full-time in character.

Limited and beset by difficulties as it is, college and university workers' education continues to grow and to make progress. This is all the more remarkable because those charged with responsibility for present programs uniformly report that they are understaffed and overworked.

Nine program directors state that they receive no administrative assistance whatsoever, another nine say that they have one administrative assistant. Two other directors have two such assistants, and another has three. One director states that he has three assistants who are half-time administrators and half-time teachers.

Full-time teachers employed by workers' education programs in

University Programs Today

institutions of higher learning are even scarcer than administrative assistants. One program reports that it has six; another that it has four. In the latter case the full-time teachers are employed largely because the program serves a large mid-western state where part-time teachers with the necessary experience and training are impossible to find except in the northeastern corner of that state.

Workers' education directors fare a bit better when it comes to secretarial help. Ten of them have their own secretaries, three have two typists in their offices, one has three, another has four, and still another has seven. Occasionally, one finds a case where a director has to struggle to get even part-time secretarial help in an emergency. The program director in a large Eastern state found himself, for reasons of economy, suddenly deprived of his secretary less than a week before he was to open a two-month program of on-campus summer schools. Only because he threatened to notify the unions which had contracted for the summer schools that he was unable to serve them, did the central administration provide him with a part-time secretary.

One director's secretary was formerly a full-time union education director who switched jobs because her husband insisted that she keep regular working hours. Another secretary is the president of an office employees' local union. Both are vitally interested in workers' education and their interest is evident in the quality of the work they do.

Although college and university workers' education programs are not liberally supplied with administrators, teachers or clerical help, generally, what they lack in quantity is made up in part by quality. Almost without exception, administrators and teachers are well trained and experienced. Clerical workers on the whole are above average and many of them take personal interest in what they are doing.

Eleven full-time administrators and teachers report that their major background is in the labor movement, an equal number indicate that the bulk of their experience was gained in the university field, four say that they have worked longest for government, and two state that they come out of management circles.

With only one or two exceptions, college and university workers' education programs depend upon carefully selected part-time teachers to give all or the greatest part of the instruction they offer. Aside from the fact that financial considerations keep most of them from putting on full-time teachers, university extension traditionally and properly, because it deals largely with practical people who have full-time jobs, relies, for teaching the bulk of its offerings, upon teachers who are top men and women in the fields of endeavor where they are regularly employed.

Reports on 297 people who currently teach part-time in these programs indicate that they are regularly employed in eight fields as follows:

Regular field of employment	Number
University	134
Labor	60
Government	46
Management	27
Law	13
Public Schools	11
Radio	4
Journalism	2
	297

While the number of people regularly employed in university work may seem high in the light of university extension policy regarding part-time teachers, one should remember that many people now working for universities, especially in the disciplines within which workers' education topics fit, have come to their present positions from years of notable accomplishment in government and other fields. A check, institution by institution, will reveal that very few men who have always been university instructors are used by workers' education programs. The management men listed are employed largely by Jesuit institutions in the field.

Of obvious significance is the report on the qualifications required of teachers in workers' education programs.

Twenty-one directors ask that instructors have experience in teaching adults; fifteen demand that instructors have experience in the labor movement. Only five require that part-time men have the A.B. degree, and just one stipulates the master's degree as a requirement. Certainly, these standards point to the functional emphasis in selection of part-time instructors. Most directors base their requirements upon practical rather than superficial standards, an approach that should be reassuring to labor.

Twenty-five directors state that they must approve all part-time teachers added to the staff. Eleven indicate that approval from the administrator to whom they are responsible is necessary. Nine must have approval from the faculty advisory committee to the program.

Compensation for part-time instructors, while not astronomic, compares very favorably with that given part-time men in other areas of university extension. Excepting the Jesuit schools, whose instructors in every instance but one are not paid, the following summarizes current part-time rates in college and university workers' education:

Compensation per hour	Number of institutions
$10 to $15	1
10	5
9	1
8	1
7.50	2
6 to 7	1
6	1
5.75	1
5	3
	16

Fifteen institutions report that they pay travel, food and lodging expenses for part-time instructors when they have to travel. Seven colleges and universities, and not in every case those which pay the highest rate per hour, state that expenses incurred by their part-time instructors must come out of their hourly compensation. The one Jesuit institution which compensates its part-time teachers solves this problem by paying five dollars per night if the assignment is local and ten dollars if travel is involved.

Despite the fact that they are extremely busy, many workers' education program administrators manage to conduct regular observations of part-time teachers. Sixteen of them state that they do this with the aim, in almost every case, of seeing each teacher at least once each academic year. In addition, twelve directors hold regular part-time teaching staff conferences largely for the purpose of evaluating the program. Six hold these conferences quarterly, two conduct them semiannually and four meet with their part-time staffs annually.

Generally, these conferences concern themselves with an examination of past experiences and practices, projected course and discussion outlines and materials, possible conference topics and conference organization, previews of audio-visual materials, and clarification and amendment of over-all philosophy and objectives.

A great deal of time and concern is given at all times by the administrative staff to the subjects discussed in these conferences. This is particularly true with regard to the supervision of materials: outlines and syllabi, books and pamphlets, and audio-visual aids.

Twenty institutions report that all outlines and syllabi used in classes and discussions must be approved by the workers' education program director. Seventeen institutions require approval by the teacher using them, eleven ask that they be passed upon by the administrator to whom the workers' education program director is responsible. Only five demand approval by the faculty advisory committee, and two require approval by the lay advisory committee.

There is somewhat less concern about books and pamphlets used in classes and discussions. Seventeen institutions ask approval by the workers' education program director, and eighteen from the teacher using them. Only seven colleges and universities demand approval from the administrator to whom the workers' education program reports, only three ask approval from the faculty advisory committee, and one asks lay advisory committee approval.

Least concern is felt for supervision of audio-visual materials. However, it should be stated that the reason largely is that not all colleges and universities use such materials in their workers' education programs. Thirteen of those which do, require the workers' education program director to preview and approve all films and filmstrips. Fifteen demand similar action on the part of teachers using the material. Four demand favorable action from the administrator to whom the workers' education director reports, none asks faculty advisory committee approval, and but one asks the lay advisory committee to pass upon films and filmstrips.

University Programs Today

Closely related to supervision is the question of liaison between college and university workers' education programs and unions.

Labor leaders and workers' education specialists in the labor movement ask such liaison both on the over-all program and direction and on specific local programs. In the first instance, they desire liaison between university and national, regional and state labor officials; in the second instance, they want it between university and appropriate local labor leaders. In both instances, the labor movement asks that there be consultation on subject matter, teaching personnel and teaching technique.

Twenty-four colleges and universities report that they consult with national, regional and state labor leaders on subject matter as it relates to over-all program and direction. Twenty institutions consult on teaching personnel in this context. Twelve institutions meet with labor to discuss teaching techniques as they relate to over-all program and direction.

Twenty-eight institutions of higher learning report that they consult with union leaders on the subject matter of the specific local program. Twenty-one say that they discuss teaching personnel locally. Fourteen meet with local labor leaders to talk over teaching technique.

While the majority of colleges and universities reporting are inclined to consult with labor on subject matter and teaching personnel, they seem much less inclined to involve themselves in possible argument over teaching technique. This probably is due largely to the fact that technique is considered a professional skill of the educator, and educators, like other professionals or skilled tradesmen, are jealous of their peculiar proficiencies.

Labor and colleges and universities are deeply interested in pre-program exploration and post-program evaluation on the local level.

The preferred practice is to set up a conference before the first session of a class, the first of a series of discussions, or before an institute. At the conference the particular needs and problems of a given union group are examined so that subsequent instruction will throw light upon those needs and problems. Participating in such conferences are the workers' education program director or his representative, the instructor who is to be assigned to the activity, and the responsible union scheduling officer.

Thirty institutions report that they attempt to hold such conferences before they begin a local program.

After a class, discussion series, or institute has been held, it is a good practice to call another conference at which the work is evaluated in terms of the objectives set at the pre-program conference. Twenty-six colleges and universities report that they hold such evaluation sessions.

Twenty-four institutions report that the workers' education program director is involved in all such evaluation meetings, twenty-one say that the responsible union scheduling officer also takes part. Only eighteen institutions require the teacher's presence, and only twelve ask that students or consumers of the program be on hand.

The apparent inclination is to let the union scheduling officer and the workers' education program director do much of the evaluating. This practice is suitable when both parties, with some measure of regularity, have attended the program being evaluated. Unfortunately this happens only infrequently. Despite the fact that it may be expensive for the university to send a part-time instructor to an evaluation meeting, and despite the fact that it may cost the union lost-time to send worker-students to such a meeting, in the long run the practice will prove to be worthwhile. Exchange of opinion between instructor and student is the best possible method of evaluation.

Findings of evaluation meetings are of value not only for future planning on a specific local level, but also for planning on a national level by the AFL and CIO education departments, international union education directors, and college and university workers' education program administrators.

These findings can be summarized with little trouble and sent along to national, regional and state union educational specialists with the general reports on activity submitted periodically by many college and university workers' education program directors to those people who are directly or indirectly responsible for educational programs in the areas where the colleges and universities function.

Twenty institutions are now making periodic reports on their workers' education activity to the appropriate union education officers on national and regional levels. Of these, six report annually, four report semiannually, two report quarterly, and eight report

University Programs Today

periodically. None of them would find it an insurmountable obstacle to add to their statistical reports the general conclusions derived from evaluation meetings held on a series of specific local workers' education programs.

Such information would be a welcome addition to data gathered by union educational specialists who have the ultimate job of seeing to it that wide programs of workers' education are carried on at the local union level by trained and experienced local union personnel.

Since twenty-six college and university workers' education program directors report that they aim for continual stimulation and strengthening of educational programs and facilities in local unions themselves, it would seem reasonable to expect that the great majority of institutions of higher learning which conduct workers' education activities would be willing to cooperate in gathering and tabulating evaluative material that would enable them and union educational specialists to do a better over-all job.

Such tabulations would be of great value particularly to those college and university workers' education programs which maintain consultation services for local unions. They would help considerably with the process of advising union education committees and executive boards as to the best methods of establishing and carrying on educational programs for their membership. Twenty-one institutions report that they now provide such consultation services.

Knowledge of general conclusions derived from evaluations of workers' education classes, discussions and institutes would be of help, too, in the promotion of workers' education services of colleges and universities. While it is true that each local union at a given time has educational problems peculiar to the situation it faces, it is also true that generally the problems of all workers and unions are similar. In any situation, those concerned can profit by knowledge of what was accomplished through education elsewhere in a similar situation. College and university workers' education programs are excellent repositories of such information.

This is especially true because workers' education programs in institutions of higher learning currently choose direct contact with union officials as the favored method of initiating educational activity for them. Twenty-eight programs report that they make their contacts with union groups through personal visits to union officials and to union meetings. Eighteen programs depend upon mail circulation of promotional literature to stimulate interest in their work. Only nine programs await requests from unions for service.

No survey of current practices of colleges and universities in workers' education would be complete without some allusion to college and university undergraduate and graduate programs in industrial relations which include curricula specifically designed to train for leadership or technical positions in the labor movement. While, strictly speaking, this is not workers' education, some institutions which conduct such programs foster a direct relationship between them and their workers' education programs, and a few of the graduates of such programs go into workers' education.

These industrial relations programs, almost all of which are of recent origin, constitute a most important phase of the workers' education and labor-management education activity for which colleges and universities and state legislatures now appropriate funds.

Thirteen colleges and universities report that they carry on training which they consider preparation for technical and leadership positions in the labor movement. This work has developed as follows:

Year program initiated	*No. of programs initiated*
1935	1
1938	1
1943	1
1944	2
1945	2
1946	2
1947	2
1948	1
1950	1
	13

Four of these thirteen institutions indicate that they make a conscious attempt to relate their resident programs to the workers' education programs carried on by their institutions. Three state that there is informal but definite contact. Six say that there is no contact between the two programs.

The institutions where planned contact is made report that they use in their programs research and teaching assistants engaged in degree work. In addition, in institutions where both formal and informal contact is established, students working for degrees sit in on workers' education activities and are assisted in making contacts with union people.

Placement in the labor movement for graduates of academic industrial relations programs is not high. Of the 875 graduates of such programs reported since 1935, only 36 have found jobs with unions.

Three institutions report that none of their graduates have found labor positions, one institution reports that it has placed 12 of its 344 industrial relations graduates in union jobs, most of the others state that they have found labor work for only two or three of the students who have passed through their hands.

Two major reasons for these low figures on placement are quite obvious. First, there still are relatively few positions in the labor movement open to "outsiders." Most unions, although there is a trend toward hiring trained technical personnel, still prefer to develop rank and file union members for positions of union leadership. Second, unions continue to be suspicious of the training colleges and universities give the full-time academic student, and they are particularly suspicious of the training given under the industrial relations heading.

Indications are that colleges and universities will continue to develop industrial relations training programs, but that few graduates of such programs will find placement in workers' education or other technical positions open in the labor movement.

5

Trends in College and University Workers' Education

WHEN A MOVEMENT DEVELops as rapidly as has college and university workers' education in the last six years, trends begin to appear.

One of the most pronounced of present trends, pointing up a broadening of content, is that toward program specialization.

Major patterns for workers' education programs have been established by six colleges and universities, and these patterns are being followed by other institutions. One university emphasizes services for workers only, another puts its major effort into promotion of improved labor-management relations, a third emphasizes separate but interrelated services for labor and management, a fourth pushes research, a fifth stresses materials, and a sixth has a primary interest in relatively long-term in-residence training.

The School for Workers at the University of Wisconsin is the outstanding example of a program set up solely to serve the peculiar needs of workers. Few colleges and universities have committed themselves philosophically to a program limited specifically to treatment of the internal and immediate needs of workers. The Wisconsin school, under the direction of the late Ernest Schwarztrauber, always was so committed.

So much has been written about the Wisconsin School for Workers that it is unnecessary to go into detail here. It is enough to say that the heart of the program is an extensive summer school development. Extension classes and discussion programs for workers during the balance of the year have had uncertain status. At times there has been appropriation for them; at other times there has not. Decision on appropriation, unfortunately, has seemed to depend more upon whether or not a given legislature was liberal or conservative than upon the needs of Wisconsin workers.

The New York State School of Industrial and Labor Relations at Cornell University, while it offers specialized adult education programs for specific labor groups, has as its major objective a much broader program geared to advancing an understanding of industrial and labor relations.

The school has three divisions: resident, research and extension, and workers' education activity is one part of the extension program. The resident program consists of four years of undergraduate study leading to the B.S. degree in industrial and labor relations, and graduate training culminating in the M.S. and Ph.D. degrees in the same field. The research division carries on research in industrial relations, provides informational services, and issues publications including a quarterly review. The extension division offers courses, discussions and institutes to management and public as well as to labor groups. The Cornell program is as broad as any thus far initiated.

Rutgers, the State University of New Jersey, through its Institute of Management and Labor Relations, puts emphasis upon extension work. The Institute is composed of four divisions, three of which are devoted to teaching. These three provide courses, discussions and institutes through separately administered but closely interrelated labor, management and public programs. The fourth division of the Institute conducts research and, through a small specialized library, offers information services to undergraduate and graduate students in various Rutgers colleges as well as to interested individuals and labor, management and public groups.

Yale University's Labor and Management Center concentrates on research into subjects of current interest and practical importance to both labor and management. It makes first-hand observations on the goals of people, including studies of their customary practices and relationships in seeking goal attainment. One study, *Why Men Do or Do Not Join Unions,* was based upon interviews held with a substantial sample of workers during and immediately following organizing campaigns in three New Haven factories. Its usefulness to union officers and organizers is obvious from its title.

The Yale center, on occasion, has conducted classes for leaders of labor and management in such subjects as Our National Economy, Collective Bargaining and Unionism, and Labor Law and Legislation. This class program, conducted two hours per week for fifteen weeks, draws most of its participants, about two-thirds management and one-third labor, from the New Haven area.[1]

The Union Leadership Training Project of the University of Chicago has built its reputation on the preparation of materials. It has prepared a general guide to discussion for workers' education specialists and course outlines, instructors' outlines and students' study guides on topics such as Collective Bargaining, Minority Problems, Labor and the Community, and Seniority Principles and Problems. Some of this material has been developed in conjunction with the educational department of the United Steelworkers of America–CIO. One course outline, that on Labor and the Community, so impressed the United Council of Churchwomen that, in cooperation with the Union Leadership Training Project, they adapted it for use with a series of regional institutes they conducted on the Church and the Community.

The Union Leadership Training Project has tested much of its workers' education material at summer schools run by labor groups and has advised labor groups on the preparation of materials.

Recently Chicago set up an eight-month Union Officers Program as part of its regular adult education activity. This program is fully accredited under social science and is a comprehensive training program for union officers. It places special emphasis on the principles and techniques of union leadership and administration in collective bargaining, membership education, and community and human relations.

1. E. Wight Bakke, *Plans and Progress* (New Haven: Yale University Labor and Management Center, 1948), pp. 17–18.

With the exception of the Harvard Trade Union Program and the Labor Education Division of Roosevelt College, this new Chicago development comes as close to a regular academic program or department devoted to workers' education as anything American colleges and universities are now doing.

The Harvard Trade Union Program, originally on a nine-month schedule, now provides an intensive thirteen-week residence course for union representatives:

> The purpose of the course is to provide training for executive responsibility, and to help Union Officers play more useful and important roles in the labor movement. The course deals with actual policy questions and decisions which confront the union leader in the discharge of his responsibilities — organizing activities, negotiation and administration of agreements, presentation of problems to government agencies and arbitrators, relations with the community, etc.[2]

The program is sponsored by the cooperating labor organizations and the Littauer School of Public Administration, the Graduate School of Business Administration, and the Department of Economics of Harvard University. Students are selected by the union which sends them, and no one is admitted to the course unless he is sent by a trade union as its representative. The program considers a record of successful experience in the labor movement as its criterion for selection of students.

These examples give an indication of the variety of specialized workers' education activities currently being conducted by colleges and universities. Other institutions very likely will develop emphases of their own. However, institutions which emphasize special aspects of workers' education will continue to find themselves concerned as well with other phases of activity in the field.

There always has been and indications are that there will continue to be a relatively high mortality rate for college and university programs in workers' education.

Lack of money heads the list of reasons for termination of workers' education programs. Columbia University's Barnard College conducted an excellent summer school for women workers during the late twenties and early thirties.[3] From 1927 to 1933, the summer

2. *Trade Union Program* (Cambridge, Massachusetts: Harvard University, 1950), p. 2.
3. *Annual Report of the Dean of Barnard College 1928* (Columbia University

school was supported largely by gifts from interested individuals. When depression struck, a $1500 subsidy from Columbia University, a large sum at the time, was not enough to keep the school functioning.[4]

State grants partially answer the problem of finance, but they are not a substitute for a strong federal aid program. Thomas E. Posey of West Virginia State College states that the workers' education program at his institution has been temporarily discontinued because the state legislature has failed to appropriate funds.[5]

What happened in West Virginia happened also in Wisconsin and will happen elsewhere so long as most states maintain inadequate tax structures and continue to elect mediocrities to state legislatures.

Another common reason for program failure is the death or transfer of one key individual responsible for workers' education activity. This apparently is more the case in Jesuit institutions than elsewhere. Brother Felix Francis of La Salle College, Philadelphia, states that "Brother Alfred . . . directed a well organized program of Workers' Education from 1935 to '43. The program was discontinued after he left."[6] Father Henry Wirtenberger of the University of Detroit reports that the death of Father Edmund Horne deprived his institution of the program's mainstay. Father Wirtenberger goes on to say that the part-time assistance of three faculty members after Father Horne's death was not enough to keep the program alive.[7] Father Wirtenberger also states that greater interest of Detroit unions in their own educational programs has, to some extent, taken the place of programs such as that run by Father Horne. He thereby pays tribute to the efforts of both the UAW–CIO and Michigan CIO Council education departments and the former staff members of the University of Michigan Workers Educational Service who, since that program's untimely demise, have offered educational services as the Workers' Education Department of the Michigan Federation of Teachers–AFL.

Father Wirtenberger also alludes to a third reason for termination of workers' education programs when he says:

> As a result of the programs carried on over a period of five years in our workers' educational program, I have developed a

Bulletin of Information Twenty-eighth Series, No. 1. New York: Columbia University, October 1, 1928), pp. 8–9.
   4. Letter from Mrs. William A. Wieners, August 21, 1950.
   5. Letter from Thomas E. Posey, June 19, 1950.
   6. Letter from Brother Felix Francis, July 10, 1950.
   7. Letter from Henry J. Wirtenberger, S.J., June 15, 1950.

major program in industrial relations in the Evening Commerce School. . . . While enrollment in our non-credit workers' educational program tapered off, we have had a steady increase of enrollees in the credit courses to the more than 200 students who are now majoring in industrial relations in the Evening Commerce School. The success of this development has lead me to believe that we can make our best contribution in this area with the resources at our disposal.[8]

While Father Wirtenberger may feel that he is making his best contribution this way, one may safely state that he is not making a workers' education contribution, if only for the reason that most workers are not eligible to take credit courses.

This statement by Father Wirtenberger demonstrates that there is very real danger of workers' education programs being replaced by labor-management education programs. This already has happened at several institutions, and others are now establishing labor-management institutes which mistakenly call part of their function workers' education. This, of course, does not mean that certain other institutions are not establishing bona fide workers' education programs within labor-management institutes — California, Illinois, Connecticut and Rutgers illustrate this development. The danger is that many colleges and universities either do not or cannot make the distinction, and label as workers' education any educational activity in which labor is invited to participate. Few are as explicit as the Industrial Relations Center at the University of Minnesota, which states:

> To avoid confusion with respect to the Center's program and workers' education, a word on that point may be appropriate. The Industrial Relations Center has neither the authority nor the facilities necessary for the provision of a comprehensive program of workers' education, which might properly include courses in many fields. The Center is concerned with but one field, that of industrial relations. Within that field, however, its resources are equally available to workers, to managements, and to any other groups interested in this area of professional training and research.[9]

One more reason for discontinuing workers' education programs is found in situations where demand is not constant and regular

8. *Ibid.*
9. *Program of the Industrial Relations Center, op. cit.*, p. 10.

programs cannot be organized. Fortunately, in some of these situations, institutions formerly more deeply involved in the field have pooled their resources. Interested faculty members at Amherst, the University of Massachusetts, Smith, and Mount Holyoke have banded together to form the Connecticut Valley University Extension Committee. Although this committee makes no effort to put its program on a regular continuing basis, it seeks, from time to time, to give classes to unionists. Small fees are charged and deficits incurred are met by the committee.[10]

The termination of workers' education activity in some institutions has been the result of decisions making educational programs for labor a part of general adult education divisions. The difficulty with this approach is that it does not allow for the peculiar status and needs of workers. Because they cannot qualify, they often are barred from credit programs. Many institutions which pontificate upon the above policy, at the same time conduct separate and specialized programs to meet the desires of business and professional groups. Labor is the one group to which they seem to apply their stated policy.

Certain colleges and universities which have attempted small beginnings in workers' education give up when they cannot find a man who in their opinion is qualified to direct such a program. The University of Toledo is looking for an individual with "both high academic training and practical business as well as teaching experience."[11] Toledo and other institutions will have to wait a long time before they find the ideal man with every possible qualification in terms of advanced degrees and field and teaching experience. Workers' education specialists are not developed as are animal husbandry specialists and doctors of philosophy. Most of them have both field and teaching experience; as yet, few of them have earned advanced degrees.

Some colleges and universities have been so involved with veterans of World War II during the past few years that they have had neither the facilities nor the staff to offer programs for union groups. The University of Alabama reports that this concern has seriously hampered summer institutes.[12]

With the exception of Alabama, which now is conducting some

10. Letter from Colston E. Warne, August 29, 1950.
11. Letter from C. K. Searles, July 13, 1950.
12. Letter from J. R. Morton, July 14, 1950.

workers' education, institutions other than those above which have dropped workers' education programs are John Carroll University of Cleveland, Ohio; University of Cincinnati; Northeastern University of Boston, Massachusetts; University of Oklahoma; St. Michael's College of Winooski, Vermont; and, of course, the University of Michigan.

A third trend in college and university workers' education is the regularity with which new institutions are entering the field.

In the spring of 1950, the University of Akron, a municipal institution, offered to workers two non-credit courses which were functional in character. One was entitled Training for the Union Officer and the other Practical Labor Law as Applicable in Akron. These courses were offered by the University's Division of Adult Education and their success has prompted the university to consider a broader program for workers.

During the winter of 1949, the Extension Division of the University of Utah conducted four classes for the Utah AFL. These classes were in part an outgrowth of a CIO Steelworkers' summer school that has been held by the university for several years. Because these activities were favorably received, the Extension Division, in the winter of 1950, set up a Labor School "to develop leadership at all levels and in every field of labor."[13]

The Akron and Utah developments illustrate how workers' education programs sometimes develop out of experimentation and expanding demand.

In 1950, after legislative authorization, the University of Puerto Rico established a Labor Relations Institute as part of its School of Public Administration. This institute will have as broad a scope as that enjoyed by the Cornell program and, as part of that scope, will offer extension instruction to trade union officers to assist them "to be efficient administrators of union affairs and to give to them and to trade union members an understanding of . . . union policy and of the role it plays in the . . . economy."[14]

Also in 1950, a Bureau of Labor and Management was set up as part of the College of Commerce of the State University of Iowa. This bureau will have two major functions: research and conference

13. *Labor School* (**Salt Lake City**, Utah: University of Utah, 1950), p. 2.
14. Letter from Labor Relations Institute, University of Puerto Rico, September 9, 1950.

planning. It probably will develop a program of workers' education should demand from labor groups make such a venture feasible.

The new Puerto Rico and Iowa agencies are illustrative of the other approach to establishment of new programs — creation by legislative or administrative act.

The University of Delaware expects to establish an Institute for Human Relations which is likely to have a program of workers' education as one of its divisions.[15] Michigan State College also is considering establishment of a workers' education program.[16]

The new development in college and university workers' education most likely to be closely watched is that in Michigan where a program sponsored directly by the State Department of Public Instruction is now underway. This program is channeled through Michigan's four teachers' colleges, Wayne University and the University of Michigan, and is supported from the general state adult education fund in terms of a minimum subsidy per class. Each participating college or university, as it develops its part in this program, will be advised by a committee of three AFL members, three CIO members, and one university representative.

Several other colleges and universities — among them Washington (St. Louis), Colorado, Maryland and Montana — which now sponsor summer institutes for specific unions or occasional extension classes during the rest of the year, are likely to continue their limited programs without any real effort to expand them. It is also likely that other colleges and universities will establish similar limited workers' education activity.

This constantly expanding college and university workers' education activity is one manifestation of the fact that the labor movement gradually is winning nationwide acceptance as a vital segment of the total community. Today colleges and universities can and should have substantial and responsible educational relationships with labor groups.

Conversely, this development means that there is increasing acceptance of college and university workers' education by the labor movement. As Mark Starr says:

> Trade unionists in the past have been in part suspicious and somewhat overawed by professors. When they meet the

---

15. Letter from Charles N. Lanier, August 17, 1950.
16. Letter from Charles C. Killingsworth, July 27, 1950.

professors man to man, they find that the majority of them realize how little they know as theoreticians and are eager to learn about the day-to-day problems of industry. Happily, too, an increasing number of educators in schools and colleges are members of the American Federation of Teachers.

They are anxious to help the trade unions to write down and interpret their industrial practices, to systematize them for the guidance of the newer generation of union members and leaders who will not need henceforth to graduate, as their predecessors literally did, from the school of hard knocks. Many of these professors already serve on wage boards and arbitration panels and are anxious to know more about unions.[17]

College and university workers' education is only now beginning to utilize the method and technique developed since 1921 by the American workers' education movement. Workers' education has always stressed the practical approach. It has always been concerned primarily with the social studies.

The bold use made by workers' education programs, both in and out of institutions of higher learning, of techniques such as role-playing, "bull-session" and "information please" points up their willingness to use every possible resource to make their offerings as meaningful as possible.

Those who are most deeply concerned about the future of adult education today are attempting to make programs for workers more meaningful and effective by closely relating study and action. Adult educators are coming to realize that the logical end of adult education is action. Yet, workers' education, because it has always been necessarily concerned with the immediate needs of labor, from the beginning has seen the relationship between study and action and has developed its method and technique accordingly.

In this connection, workers' education has maintained a close relationship with progressive education and educators. It has therefore been able to maintain a forward-looking and, on occasion, quite radical approach to educational theory and practice.

Workers' education has constantly attempted to develop new methods and new organizations of subject matter. Its curricula are

17. Mark Starr, *Workers' Education* (New York: International Ladies Garment Workers Union, 1943), p. 1.

in a constant process of readjustment and it is alert to redefine its objectives when that is necessary.

Another trend in college and university workers' education is increased emphasis on broadening the areas of activity.

With very few exceptions, existing programs are beginning to embrace a three-fold function. They attempt to help the worker become a fuller and more integrated individual, a more active and responsible member of his union, and a participating citizen in his community.

Unions today are assisting workers with out-plant as well as in-plant problems. College and university programs are helping them, for example, by giving instruction on interviewing and referral techniques in union counseling courses. Greater use is being made of such films as "Your Children and You," "Feeling of Rejection," and "Life With Grandpa" as part of discussions for workers. More and more frequently, college and university programs list courses in and conferences on human relations and practical psychology.

It is no accident that most college and university programs conduct courses concerned with the human and social implications of collective bargaining as well as those concerned with the economic facts of collective bargaining. While core titles like Collective Bargaining and Negotiations and Grievances have retained their popularity, courses in Health, Welfare and Pension Plans, Time Study, Job Evaluation, Labor Economics, Labor Problems and Arbitration — courses which make the union officer and the union steward much better able to hold their own with management — are being offered more frequently. There is broad treatment of the background, skills and techniques needed to make active union members better able to fulfill their responsibilities and obligations.

Unions more than ever are concerning themselves with community affairs and problems. College and university programs now offer a whole category of courses and other educational activities dealing with community and public relations, labor and government, international labor affairs, unemployment and workmen's compensation, and cooperatives and credit unions. Every indication is that increasing emphasis will be put upon this kind of offering by established workers' education programs in our institutions of higher learning. Union members are learning to be participating citizens in their communities, and training programs will step up this process.

In some areas, real attention is being given to relationships between farmers and workers. Goddard College in Vermont for several years has sponsored meetings of farm and labor representatives to discuss common problems. One meeting considered establishment of consumer cooperatives through the joint efforts of farmers and such labor groups as the quarry and textile workers.

Both the AFL and CIO and many international unions affiliated with them have established anti-discrimination departments, international relations departments, community services departments and other specialized divisions dealing specifically with defined areas of community living. None of these units is either over-staffed or over-financed. All of them need assistance from college and university workers' education programs which have easy access to local specialists who can help make clear to workers the problems all citizens face in these specialized areas.

Colleges and universities, through their workers' education programs, can and do offer worthwhile services to the worker as an individual, as a union member, and as a citizen. They will one day make their major contribution in helping to develop in workers and union officials broader understanding of the economic, political and social issues facing us.

Despite occasional contrary experiences like those cited by Fathers Wirtenberger and Brown, the trend is in the direction of more workers' education activity within labor-management programs, and not in the direction of more labor-management education in workers' education programs.

Programs like those at Cornell and Connecticut, which started out with emphasis on classes open to labor, management and the public, and which now offer both these so-called community type classes and specialized activities tailored to fit the needs of specific labor and management groups, are finding that the latter kind of activity has been given the warmest welcome and that the demand for it is growing rapidly.

The major reason why colleges and universities have placed workers' education activities within the framework of labor-management institutes is fear of management and community disapproval of education frankly for workers only. While some institutions of higher learning have rationalized that both labor and management must benefit from whatever specialized service is established, none has yet been able to answer labor's charge that, in most institutions, management already is being adequately served through schools and colleges of commerce and business administration, and that creation of a labor-management institute almost always provides duplicative services and jurisdictional problems within the university. With the exception of Roosevelt College, Chicago, which has a Labor Education Division equal in status to the other divisions of the college, no college or university has had the interest or courage to set up a fully-manned and fully-financed workers' education department.

However, the present trend is away from timidity. As programs of labor-management institutes have developed, as top administrators have had the peculiar problems of labor explained to them by workers' education specialists in their employ and by lay labor members of their advisory committees, they have broadened their programs to reach those internal and immediate needs of labor the satisfaction of which is a prerequisite to the improvement of industrial relations.

In all but a few cases, the original reluctance to stand up to those who for selfish reasons want to push back or at least contain workers' education was the product of ignorance rather than intent.

The trend within labor-management institutes definitely is toward broad workers' education programs as part of their function.

Because the job before workers' education is both extensive and complex, because the wealth of experience, skill and technique developed by the American workers' education movement since 1921 is still little understood or appreciated within the college and university sphere, because college and university workers' education programs develop pragmatically, experimentation is a trend that will continue.

On the extension front, any attempt now to limit the "proper" content of workers' education offerings would be both regrettable and premature. The labor movement has a wide and growing variety of interests and needs. College and university workers' education programs should remain relatively unstructured and free to meet them.

Only one institution of higher learning today offers a course labeled Political Action for Unions; nine offer courses called Labor and Government. Only one institution currently offers a course entitled How to Organize; twenty-six offer courses headed Steward Training. Only a few years ago, most institutions would have given a course entitled Political Science but not one called Labor and

Government. Only a few years ago, most institutions would have scheduled a course labeled Collective Bargaining but not one called Steward Training. Before long, even though such classes might be better handled within the labor movement itself, classes in Political Action for Unions and How to Organize probably will be as commonplace in college and university workers' education offerings as are Labor and Government and Steward Training classes today. The trend is toward broader recognition of the specific problems facing labor. Just as institutions of higher learning have offered to doctors and bankers courses specifically dealing with their peculiar problems, eventually they will give labor the same specialized service.

College and university workers' education programs utilize classes, film and lecture discussions, on- and off-campus day-long and weekend institutes and on-campus summer schools as settings for their offerings. The trend is toward increased use of every one of these media by most institutions. While classes will probably continue to be the most extensive offering, more and more institutions will begin or expand particularly experimental use of the other media. As old techniques of informal adult education are rediscovered or reemphasized and as new techniques are developed, college and university workers' education will use them boldly.

Teaching personnel for college and university workers' education is part-time and is selected on the basis of "who is best qualified to do this specific job at this particular time." The two criteria used most frequently are experience in teaching adults and experience in the labor movement. Large groups of teachers will continue to come out of government work, although the trend is toward the hiring of more qualified men from within the labor movement.

Colleges and universities are learning that if a man is competent in his field of specialization, if he is gifted at teaching adults, if he has knowledge and sympathetic understanding of the labor movement, the fact that he may be employed by a labor union is a welcome further qualification.

The trend is toward experimentation with subject matter, with teaching technique, and with teaching personnel.

In the latter area it is worth noting that, more and more, college and university workers' education programs are concerned with teacher training. One or two institutions not necessarily desirous of conducting expansive extension programs might well give their attention to the training of workers' education specialists. Many institutions will offer courses and other activities designed to develop the local union education committee function and educational leadership techniques.

The CIO Department of Education and Research long has had an excellent film department. For some months now the Workers Education Bureau–AFL has concerned itself with informing affiliated unions of good audio-visual equipment and materials, and the Bureau has established a film library. Many international union education departments, both AFL and CIO, have established film divisions — the International Chemical Workers–AFL and the United Automobile Workers–CIO have particularly active ones.

In addition, both national federations of labor and many international unions have begun to produce films and filmstrips on their own activities and those of the labor movement in general.

The trend very definitely is toward increased production and utilization of audio-visual materials — charts and turnover talks as well as films and filmstrips. The workers' education program in a college or university usually is either part of or directly connected with the extension division, which, as is generally true, maintains an extensive audio-visual department. It is therefore reasonable to suppose that workers' education programs will with increasing frequency turn to these audio-visual departments for material.

Unhappily, proper use of films and filmstrips at the local union level remains the exception rather than the rule. When most unions plan to show a film, theirs is a literal intent. The film showing rarely is preceded by an introduction and rarely is followed by discussion. Many times the film is scheduled an hour or so before the regular meeting time and the prospective audience, used to the regular time, arrives too late to see it. On other occasions a film is placed at the very bottom of the agenda and the audience, suffering from debate fatigue, either drifts out or sleeps.

Yet the trend is toward greater use of audio-visual aids. Fortunately, there is an equally pronounced trend on the part of college and university workers' education programs to prepare discussion outlines for the films they use and to send films and filmstrips out only when accompanied by these outlines and a trained discussion leader.

Certain institutions also are beginning to conduct audio-visual workshops both as extension activities on a year-round basis and as part of summer schools and regional institutes. This means that college and university workers' education will assist local union education committees to develop film and filmstrip discussions that are properly planned and executed.

6

Areas of Operation for College and University Workers' Education

ALMOST ALL WORKERS' EDUcation programs at the college and university level established since 1944, in relative terms the period of great expansion, have been organized as divisions of institutes or schools of industrial or labor-management relations.

This practice, which probably already is a principle, will win acceptance from the labor movement only to the extent that these divisions are permitted to take the functional approach to workers' education. The functional approach requires that primary emphasis now be put upon an attempt to help labor understand its own needs and problems.

Survey and experience indicate that the necessity for this functional approach is understood by many institutes of labor-management relations which offer workers' education activities.

This does not mean that workers' education programs within these schools or institutes will entirely replace, are superior to, or should prevent the establishment of, solely workers' education agencies on college and university campuses. It does mean that this approach to workers' education at the college and university level is working out successfully and very likely will be utilized by most institutions of higher learning which decide to enter the field.

Whatever their administrative organization, functional workers' education programs will assist unions to attain the knowledge, skills and techniques which will enable their representatives to bargain in an informed and intelligent manner. They also will concern themselves with the human and social implications of collective bargaining as well as with its economic facts. In other words, they will transcend the narrow limits that strict constructionists in industrial relations education would impose upon them. They constantly will expand and broaden their offerings.

Colleges and universities will continue to provide direct services of many types as long as labor needs them. These services will have to develop what Mark Starr calls the "Three D's" — discipline, directive and dynamic — and will have to be provided by agencies either directly engaged in or actively working with other appropriate agencies engaged in the four areas of workers' education listed by John Dunlop and James Healy.

Dunlop and Healy say that training for rank and file workers should be conducted by the labor movement itself and by university extension; training for stewards and officers should also be conducted by these two agencies; training for technicians — lawyers, doctors, economists, etc. — should be conducted by our regular professional schools; and that training for staff officers — the emerging labor "professionals" — should be conducted by resident, in-service, highly specialized and advanced training programs such as that at Harvard.[1]

Within each of these four broad divisions of function, very specific types of activity will have to be developed and encouraged.

The 668 extension classes, 915 lecture and film discussions, 78 off-campus conferences and institutes, and 15 summer school programs conducted by colleges and universities during the academic year 1949–1950 reached a total of only 50,690 workers. In terms of the potential among 16,000,000 organized workers alone, this is an extremely limited showing when we consider that it represents a real

1. John T. Dunlop and James J. Healy, "The University's Contribution to Advanced Labor Education," *Journal of Educational Sociology*, 20:472–75, April, 1947.

increase in the amount of workers' education activity conducted by institutions of higher learning. When we consider further that, even with the increase, colleges and universities are able to satisfy only the most urgent demand, we have some idea of the reception unions will give to vastly expanded college and university workers' education programs.

Direct services of this kind are extension activities. Programs now operating them unanimously indicate that they will be continued and expanded as colleges and universities get the necessary funds.

However, neither expansion of university services of this kind nor expansion of similar services provided by union education departments can ultimately satisfy the demand. The real job has to be done at the local union level by local union people specially trained to do it. It is for this reason that college and university workers' education programs will have to accept more responsibility for advising local union officers and education committees on planning and executing educational activities for their memberships. By expanding this educational counseling function, they will help bring about the transfer of responsibility for direct services to the local unions themselves.

It should be part of their counseling function for colleges and universities to point out to union people the many other programs, both civic and cultural, that are part of general university extension, and to explain the assistance available to local unions, once they learn how to look for it, from public schools, libraries, museums and other community agencies which either directly or indirectly perform educational functions.

The preparation of material is one specific direct service which colleges and universities should provide for unions interested in workers' education. The need for material stands out clearly; it has been apparent to both union and university workers' education specialists since the early days of the American workers' education movement.

J. B. S. Hardman, former education director of the Amalgamated Clothing Workers–CIO, says that the "tools" which the "industry" has developed are inadequate for the job.[2] Dr. Mollie Ray Carroll states that "Search for adequate teaching materials has turned up a demand for special research."[3]

2. Hardman, *op. cit.*, p. 12.
3. Carroll, *op. cit.*, p. 497.

Areas of Operation

Kermit Eby says that "The time has come for all of us in workers' education . . . to put greater emphasis on content and less on techniques."[4]

Dealing with hastily prepared mimeographed materials and hurriedly written pamphlet simplifications of primary sources which have replaced the earlier Workers' Bookshelf of the Workers Education Bureau, T. R. Adam says:

> At the present moment, workers' education throughout the country is somewhat in the position of a college whose library consists almost wholly of sets of theses by its own graduate students.[5]

A short-lived partial answer to this problem of materials was provided during most of 1947 when a small Labor Education Service existed as part of the Division of Labor Standards of the U. S. Department of Labor. This service was headed, on a part-time basis, by Arthur A. Elder.

The service was designed to promote amicable industrial relations through the encouragement of voluntary programs of workers' education directed toward the training of capable union leaders and the development of workers well informed as to the rights and responsibilities of unionism. It offered assistance with the development of workers' education programs on the local level, prepared teaching outlines and study guides, made beginnings toward the creation of an information and research service for union educational agencies, provided technical consultants and conference leaders, and printed, for a short time, a monthly *Labor Education News* which carried articles by workers' education specialists, summaries of current activity in the field, and bibliographies.

During one of the periodic economy drives that hit the labor department rather frequently during the immediate post-World War II days, the service lost its appropriation and disappeared. Several times since its disappearance, the creation of a similar agency as a substitute for a federal labor extension agency has been broached, particularly at times when labor extension legislation seemed to be completely bogged down. Naturally, such a service is no substitute

---
4. Kermit Eby, "General Education for Economic Well-Being" (unpublished article written 1949), p. 8.
5. Adam, *op. cit.*, p. 122.

for the kind of broad program envisioned by those who have supported labor extension, and the idea has never taken hold.

One other answer to this problem of materials lies within the bounds of college and university workers' education programs. Steps on the exchange of materials have been taken by the twelve union and university people who are consultants to the University of Chicago workers' education program. This activity should be expanded to include all workers' education specialists in colleges and universities who could make contributions.

Anyone who examines the Steelworkers' Institute notebooks put out by Illinois or Penn State, the notebook of the California State Federation of Labor Asilomar Institute put out by California, or the Chemical Workers' notebook put out by Rutgers, knows that there is a wealth of source material developed by college and university summer school programs.

Extension and research bulletins issued by Cornell, Yale, Minnesota and other institutions are another source of useful material.

Labor and Public Relations conference summaries available through Rutgers, and Labor Editors Conference proceedings distributed by Illinois are examples of the kind of material on specific problems currently being assembled by workers' education at the university level.

Finally, course outlines and materials prepared by almost every college and university program in the field would be extremely useful to any local union interested in attempting to begin workers' education activities.

However, such materials should not be broadcast indiscriminately where there is no previous experience with workers' education. In the beginning stages, the material should be made available in conjunction with the educational consultation service most college and university workers' education programs now are offering the labor movement. This procedure is doubly advisable because, through discussion between union and university, material could be tailored to the specific needs and problems of the labor group requesting assistance. So that proper liaison can be maintained, union education departments, wherever possible, should be directly involved in these consultations and always should be kept informed of the results that come from them.

Areas of Operation

The selection of teachers is a particularly crucial problem in workers' education. The successful teacher in the field combines a thorough knowledge of subject matter, practical experience in the labor movement, and the ability to work congenially with adult workers. College and university workers' education programs use part-time people almost entirely, and there is not a single such program which today says that it has an adequate supply of good teachers.

There are three areas in which colleges and universities can train teachers.

First, quarterly or even more frequent in-service training institutes or conferences should be conducted for part-time teachers. These meetings should deal with clarification and embellishment of proven techniques in workers' education and instruction on new techniques, and should include previews of new films and filmstrips and discussion of other audio-visual aids. As a long-range objective, each college and university program should aim at developing what might be called a permanent part-time staff of its most successful teachers. These people should be paid a guaranteed minimum yearly compensation and should be ready on call to meet to share each other's teaching skills and techniques.

Second, every college and university workers' education program ought to offer training in the techniques of educational leadership to union groups. This training should be offered in regular extension classes, as a topic of regional off-campus conferences and institutes, and as one of several courses offered at on-campus labor summer schools. Participants in this educational leadership training should be carefully selected. Enrollment should be limited to members of union education committees and other union officials specifically charged with, and with some talent for, the educational function. The training should be basic in character, dealing with such things as discussion leadership and proper use of films and filmstrips. A few college and university programs already are providing such training through classes, off-campus institutes and summer schools.

Third, more highly specialized and long-range training should be offered to established and potential union educational leaders, particularly by those colleges and universities which do not themselves expect to conduct expansive and ambitious general workers' education extension programs. Programs like those offered by the Union Leadership Training Project at the University of Chicago and the Trade Union Program at Harvard University could well give thorough educational leadership training to selected union officials either on long-term in-service or short-term residence bases. Trainees could then go back to their areas of operation and develop other people at the regional and local levels.

The in-service teacher training programs suggested above will be difficult to establish on the requisite scale. It will be infinitely more difficult, however, eventually to establish a degree program in workers' education. No union today can afford to send any of its leaders even for in-service training on anything but a short-term basis. It was for this reason that the Harvard Trade Union Program was cut from nine to three months. Established union leaders never will be able to leave their jobs long enough to do extensive full-time resident degree work, no matter how valuable that training might be. As Mark Starr says, "It is utopian to think that union representatives can be released from their day-to-day responsibilities for a period of four years to graduate as labor leaders."[6] Besides, union officers and educational specialists tend to favor short-term extension programs over both short- and long-term residence programs, considering the former to be more realistic and closer to the job and the union.

Yet we cannot afford to forget that a workers' education program worthy of the name eventually should provide research and resident instruction as well as extension and short-term on-campus training. What has been started within the Labor Education Division at Roosevelt College may be the beginning of this broader program.

Fannia Cohn has given us an idea of the complexity of the job of today's union leader, and all indications are that that job will become more rather than less complex. Certainly labor should be interested in making it possible for capable young people to be prepared particularly for professional and technical jobs within the labor movement.

The many scholarships open to the sons and daughters of workers that labor groups now are sponsoring at various colleges and universities is one evidence that unions are awakening to the need. The one-year work-school training program initiated by the International Ladies Garment Workers Union–AFL (and soon to be expanded)

6. Mark Starr, "Unions Look at Education in Industrial Relations," *Journal of Educational Sociology*, 20:501, April, 1947.

is another such evidence. But these programs and others like them are not enough. Nor is it enough to say that unions will continue to derive the bulk of their future leadership from the ranks in mine, mill and shop.

The leader who emerges from the ranks soon finds himself in the position of being unable to take time for study from his regular work. College or university training for labor positions either through our present regular collegiate curricula or through one-year programs such as that now offered by the ILGWU will never be broad nor long enough to be adequate to the need.

What we really must have is a full curriculum within a department of workers' education such as that envisioned by Theodore Brameld and George Counts.[7] Such a department within a college or university would be the equal in personnel and facilities to any other regular department within an institution of higher learning and would offer four full years of training for carefully selected candidates.

In order to assure proper student selection and to safeguard the purposes of the workers' education department, all departmental plans would have to be discussed and established through the joint action of departmental personnel and representatives of the labor movement. It would have to be remembered that the principal purpose of a major in workers' education would be to train for technical, professional and eventually leadership positions in the labor movement.

Naturally, the planners would be aware that in no field are leaders manufactured artificially. A fresh graduate in workers' education would be no more likely to step into a position of major responsibility than is the present graduate in business administration. However, the presumption is that he would in time be more ready for such responsibility than one who had not met the qualifications which graduation from a workers' education department would require.

Teachers for this proposed workers' education department would be selected only after extensive search. They would submit not only thorough training in the social sciences, philosophy and education, but also practical experience in the labor movement and workers' education activities.

7. Counts and Brameld, *op. cit.*, pp. 273–76.

Student specialization within the department would vary according to the types of positions open in the labor movement. Some would prepare to become organizers, others business agents, some editors, others teachers. Teachers for workers' education activities at local and regional levels would be trained to understand the art of educating adult workers just as carefully and thoroughly as kindergarten or homemaking instructors are trained today. Knowledge of the subject matter of the field, psychology, methods, educational theory and statistics all would be imparted.

Besides the various types of specialized training, every student in workers' education would get sound grounding in the social, philosophical and psychological foundations of education. He would pursue a core of studies revolving around the economic, political and social issues which face society at any given time. One part of this study would consist of a central seminar where experts from the social sciences, art, philosophy, science, agriculture and business would examine society's problems with the students. This problem examination would include actual contact with community agencies and resources such as factories, union offices, settlement houses, welfare departments, hospitals, etc.

Preferably, the program would be of the work-study type, affording students opportunity to interne in their fields of special interest while completing their formal studies.

A composite pattern of the workers' education department of a college or university would include in addition to full-time resident work-study programs, statewide extension services to labor: extension classes, on-campus conferences, regional off-campus institutes, and summer schools.

Research into general problems facing the labor movement, research into special problems facing specific labor groups, and provision of a general informational service to the labor movement also should be included as part of the function of the workers' education department.

Obviously, public colleges and universities would be the logical homes of such departments of workers' education as are envisioned here. If schools or departments of engineering, law, medicine, journalism, agriculture or commerce now prepare young men and women at public expense for professional or business life, similar schools or departments especially devoted to the training of new leadership for the labor movement would be entirely legitimate and a proper extension of the many services now offered the community by public institutions of higher learning.

In fact, if colleges and universities do not accept their responsibility in this field, they are remiss. Collective bargaining, if it is to work, requires equal knowledge and training on the part of both parties concerned. Actual and potential problems in our highly complex and dynamic society make the democratic operation of trade unions essential. Labor, increasingly a force in the modern community, must have the same opportunities for development through education that now are accorded other important segments of our society.

In the long run, training for future leaders of unions is at least equally as important as the maintenance and extension of educational services to adult workers which is the immediate concern of college and university workers' education. It is for this reason that such training cannot be omitted from a discussion of college and university workers' education today.

No modern institution is more adequately equipped to carry on research than is the college or university. It has resources, staff, and is in a position to secure grants from both unions and foundations for specific projects it wishes to undertake.

Particularly in recent years, colleges and universities have interested themselves in general labor problems. The Yale Labor-Management Center made a study of reasons why workers join unions. Minnesota's Industrial Relations Center is examining the effects on the community of certain common union practices. Illinois' Institute of Industrial and Labor Relations, as part of its Decatur study, is determining the impact of a local labor movement on a community over a period of years. Rutgers' Institute of Management and Labor Relations has made a study of the reaction of unions in New Jersey to escalator clauses in union contracts.

These are examples of general labor research of a type that will be continued and expanded. Actually, the work is just getting underway.

Again because they have staff, resources and access to foundation and other grants, colleges and universities are admirably fitted to conduct experimentation in the field of workers' education.

Program specialization such as that we have examined is partially experimentation, but in itself it is not enough.

In the first place, the task of workers' education is so extensive and complex that programs whose sole purpose is experimentation must be encouraged and developed. Most current college and university workers' education programs have to show results and satisfy demand if they are to meet labor's needs. They do not have available time to conduct purely exploratory experimentation.

In the second place, in one very real sense it is in the experimental approach that the greatest hope of workers' education lies. At its best, it is free of the dead hand of tradition and has the flexibility and power of adjustment necessary to get things done.

In the third place, if workers' education is eventually to get the state and federal funds essential if it is to satisfy demand, experimentation alone will provide the many effective lines of action that will convince skeptics of the ability of workers' education to do the gigantic job it faces.

It is imperative that reports on the development and results of experimentation be made available to everyone in the field. A central agency where this pooled information is available must be provided.

Survey, correspondence, conversations and experience indicate that college and university workers' education will continue to expand and broaden direct services to unions, training of workers' education teachers, and programs of research and experimentation. There is some evidence that it will institute degree programs for specialists of various types needed by the labor movement. These are the major areas of operation for workers' education programs, areas presenting problems which need further extensive study.

Unions would like to know how to get more representative and more intelligent participation, not only in classes, conferences and summer schools conducted by college and university workers' education programs, but also in union meetings and other union activities of all kinds. This concern over participation is an old problem not at all peculiar to labor situations, but a common problem of organizations of all kinds.

As Professor Wilbur C. Hallenbeck of Teachers College, Columbia University, has pointed out, we have made progress with this problem, but we have by no means solved it. We have studied techniques of publicity and promotion and have found that they help, but with limitations. We have explored the interests and needs of adults and have made some progress in reorienting our concepts of adult education to square with our findings. We have acquired knowledge about the psychology of the adult and have analyzed the implications for

Areas of Operation

adult education methods, but we have not put these implications fully into practice because of the difficulty involved in getting teachers. We have increased our skill in discussion. We have recognized the relationship between adult education and action, but we are just beginning to understand how to mesh the two. We have explored the group process and have begun to see the potentialities of group dynamics. We have found and are continuing to find a connection between adult education and the extension of democracy. Yet participation is still a major problem.[8]

At the root of this problem is the fact that, because of increasing urbanization, success remains an individual matter and living remains compartmentalized. For example, when a union organizes a plant, the appeal is made in terms of what the individual can expect from a successful organizing campaign. And any union official will admit that a union meeting at which a proposed wage increase is under discussion is certain to be a crowded meeting. The conclusion has to be that participation expands only under stress or when individual success is in jeopardy. Obviously, participation due solely to probable individual gain is not participation of the best kind and will hardly lead toward the extension of democracy.

Professor Hallenbeck suggests that we attack the problem by helping people gain community experience. Within this framework, he says, people can discover at first hand that others have the same problems and that their common problems can be solved by co-operative action. He also contends that people should be involved in terms of needs as they see them, not as we see them — a good workers' education practice — and he cautions that we should not expect too much, that we should realize that potentialities for participation in any single program or organization are limited.[9]

Professor Hallenbeck has summarized the problem of participation in admirable fashion. Future studies of college and university workers' education should extend investigation along the lines he suggests.

College and university workers' education programs should consider seriously the requests from unions for specific research into the problems those unions face. Unions need evaluation of some of the

---

8. Wilbur C. Hallenbeck, "Diagnosis of the Problem of Participation" (unpublished paper read before annual meeting of American Association for Adult Education, Cleveland, May 4, 1950), pp. 1–2.
9. *Ibid.*, pp. 4–6.

materials they have been using. Are comic books effective when they deal with such problems as discrimination? Do people read the pamphlets on union problems published by colleges and universities and union education and research departments? Are vocabulary levels in such pamphlets correct? Do films and filmstrips really help in union educational situations?

There are all kinds of problems facing the modern union as its function becomes more and more complex. What are the difficulties likely to be encountered by a union in a given shop or series of shops in an industry which may decide to use time and motion study or job evaluation on a large scale? What kind of improved health and welfare plan or pension plan would best fit the employees of a particular mill or group of mills who are covered by a contract which includes provision for such a plan?

Many unions facing these and similar highly technical problems are asking college and university workers' education programs for research assistance which so far is not forthcoming on the necessary scale. Future studies of college and university workers' education might project methods for such research.

Further research into the problems and practices of college and university workers' education is another need and one which existing programs can help satisfy with a minimum of internal clearance.

First and foremost of needs in this area is that relating to collection of more facts on finance. Our survey has indicated that little information is available on appropriations for college and university workers' education, fees charged by institutions now conducting programs, and costs of the various workers' education activities regularly scheduled today by colleges and universities.

There should be available much more information about the reasons which prevent more than seven colleges and universities from developing workers' education programs frankly oriented toward satisfaction first of the primary and internal needs of workers.

Additional study should be given to the proper division of function between labor-conducted and college- and university-conducted workers' education. What services and activities can best be supplied by institutions of higher learning; what services and activities should be furnished solely by the labor movement?

Colleges and universities have produced a few films and filmstrips specifically for use in the field of workers' education. Also, through

Areas of Operation

preparation of mimeographed discussion outlines, they have adapted audio-visual aids only indirectly related to topics of interest to workers. A future study might deal with the extent to which college and university workers' education programs should involve themselves with the production and improvement of audio-visual media.

Research in the whole field of evaluative procedure as it can be applied specifically to workers' education is a particularly urgent need. Similar research is needed in the area of teaching methods and techniques.

One very much neglected area is that of the history of the American workers' education movement. The experience of the movement since 1921 should be assembled through thorough research and disseminated throughout the present movement. Specifically, the WPA workers' education program experience, which is altogether too little known, should be brought together in a readable account.

Colleges and universities interested either in continuing or beginning to operate workers' education programs, and individuals or groups planning to carry on research dealing with the many vexing problems these institutions of higher learning face or will face, should benefit from a statement of the essentials of an effective college and university workers' education program.

7

The Functional Approach to College and University Workers' Education

WORKERS' EDUCATION IS AN essential function of college and university adult education. Through their extension divisions, institutions of higher learning play an important role in the development of the American workers' education movement.

History records past contributions of colleges and universities in the field. Survey and experience attest to their relatively expansive current workers' education offerings. The probability of increased state aid and at least the beginnings of federal aid to workers' education indicates that these offerings are likely to be both expanded and broadened.

However, organized labor and higher education are aware that even expanded and broadened programs never will attain maximum effectiveness until the role of colleges and universities in workers' education is defined to the satisfaction of both.

A statement of the essentials of an effective college and university

The Functional Approach

workers' education program which would be acceptable to both parties should serve to define that role. A functional approach is the first essential of an effective college and university workers' education program.

History and current activities demonstrate that workers' education conducted by American institutions of higher learning is not class education. In common with labor-conducted workers' education in this country, it is a development indigenous to the American scene rather than foreign preparation for revolution. It fits smoothly into the context of an evolving capitalism under which industrial relations will be as stable as is consistent with the freedom of choice and enterprise inherent in the system.

Of necessity, therefore, effective college and university workers' education is too realistic to hold a preconceived notion that the only lack in industrial relations is opportunity for labor and management to sit down together calmly in a classroom atmosphere out of which stable industrial relations will evolve. It contends that collective bargaining problems are settled at the bargaining table rather than in the classroom. The function of the workers' education classroom, when dealing with the employment contact, is to give labor the knowledge, skills and techniques that will enable its representatives to bargain in an informed and intelligent manner. In addition, even in the employment contact context, the effective workers' education program concerns itself with the human and social implications of collective bargaining as well as with its economic facts. It realizes that out-plant problems of workers are as important as, and effect collective bargaining as much as, in-plant problems.

Whether independent or a part of an industrial relations or labor-management school or institute, the effective college and university workers' education program is concerned with much more than the employment contact. It endeavors to make the worker a better person, a more effective member of his union group, and a participating citizen in his community. It is designed to enable workers to understand their own experiences and problems. It conducts workers' education activities with the aim of assisting workers with their felt needs, problems and interests.

This functional approach, which asks what labor wants and expects before it attempts to provide answers, has been long in developing. It has evolved as a synthesis of the intellectualism that quarantined early attempts to provide workers' education, and the practicality that excluded all but the affairs of the moment and was characteristic of the intermediate level of philosophic formulation in workers' education. It is empirical rather than positive in outlook. It attempts to provide broad economic, political and social background as well as practical "bread and butter" skills and techniques. But it provides both in the context of felt needs and interests in a given area at a given time.

Early nineteenth century attempts to provide workers' education programs were sponsored and executed by German, French, English and American intellectuals and social reformers who worked on, rather than with, the labor movement. They had no base of mass support for their theories, and they failed.

With the founding of the American Federation of Labor and the enunciation of Samuel Gompers' philosophy of practicality, workers' education became totally concerned with immediate craft problems. Development and extension of programs of vocational education was one manifestation of this concern. Labor made an abrupt about-face in its policy on workers' education.

When the American workers' education movement came into being in 1921, there were evident efforts to synthesize the intellectual and practical aspects of workers' education on what has since been developed as a functional basis.

While this synthesis has been established, it is still evolving and we are still concerned with bringing together daily practice and recrystallized beliefs.

This evolving functional approach to college and university workers' education at present is not acceptable to many leaders of American management and to the college and university trustees and pedagogues whom they are able to influence. These people suspect the motives of the American labor movement. Their suspicions lead them to attempt to claim stewardship over college and university educational activity planned specifically for workers. They try to place this activity under the general supervision of schools of commerce or business administration whose traditional and primary function is to serve business and industry. They emphasize the need for labor to appreciate management's problems. They think in terms of labor-management education rather than in terms of workers' education.

The Functional Approach

These people insist that classes and other college and university workers' education activities should be mixed — should be open to both labor and management. What they fail to see is that, from the point of view of sound educational tradition and experience, the most effective teaching is done in the friendly atmosphere of an homogeneous group with a common background of experience and training.

Experience shows that improved industrial relations grow out of a democratic balance between functioning equals, and such a balance, in turn, grows out of an internally healthy trade unionism which is achieved only by direct educational service to labor in terms of labor's own needs and interests. Hilda Smith has this to say about special programs and classes for labor:

> The answer to this question of the critics is to be found in any discussion by workers themselves of what they want in education and why they want it. To them, and to students of education and of community organization, it is apparent that too often groups concerned with the organized labor movement have been excluded from opportunities to use community resources. Sometimes, it is true, workers have excluded themselves, because of their lack of self-confidence when they mingle with people of more obvious educational advantages. Sometimes there are other obstacles: it is a long trip to classes; carfare is lacking; the building available for the class is too formal in its atmosphere. And too often, as many workers have said, the teacher or leader, unaware of the strong natural interests of the workers' group, either opposes the discussion of the very question that the workers themselves are eager to discuss, or else, in their own words, "The teacher doesn't know as much about these questions as we do."
>
> . . . For what these workers desire is free and full discussion in simple terms of the matters that are of prime concern to them — their jobs, their union, their everyday problems.[1]

A survey of and experience with joint labor-management classes indicate that many workers, as Miss Smith says, lose self-confidence when they meet educationally with people who have had past educational advantages. Usually in such cases the workers "clam up" or become defensively aggressive. With either reaction it should be

1. Hilda W. Smith, "New Directions in Workers' Education," *Journal of Adult Education*, 12: 165–66, April, 1940.

obvious that nothing is accomplished in the improvement of industrial relations. In fact, the clouded climate is further beclouded. The end result is that "rank-and-file union members simply do not attend typical university extension courses in industrial relations."[2]

Moreover, if institutions of higher learning were to apply the same rule to management groups now demanding joint or open workers' education classes, there would be an immediate falling off of interest in extension courses now conducted for those groups on a closed basis. Recently the head of a workers' education program at a large eastern state college was told that representatives of one of the country's most powerful railroads were urging the open class policy for his program. When he replied that he would be glad to initiate such a policy if that railroad would open supervisory classes to members of the railroad unions, the original request was promptly dropped.

If the functional approach to workers' education is taken, officers and non-commissioned officers necessary for an evolving, advancing and ever more responsible labor movement can be trained, and this kind of labor movement of itself will contribute to the improvement of industrial relations.

Many who insist upon joint educational activities are motivated by a groundless fear that classes for workers alone will promote the class struggle concept. What, apparently, they do not understand is that labor leaders and older and more thoughtful union members (who comprise the majority in organized labor) are committed to a policy of gradual adjustment — they are not flaming revolutionaries. These people want a prosperous industry so that they can share in its gains. They want to contribute their knowledge and experience to the solving of the problems of our economic system and society. But, for the most part, they are people of little formal education or training. Selected mainly for standing out in union meetings and for shrewdness in negotiating with employers, they are intuitive and pragmatic and often have to learn through the process of trial and error. They realize that workers' education activities will give them training in social and economic analysis and will make them better leaders, better able to command willing and intelligent rank and file cooperation for their common sense programs.

---

2. Baldwin M. Woods and Abbott Kaplan, "Areas and Services of University Extension in Industrial Relations Programs," *Journal of Educational Sociology*, 20: 486–87, April, 1947.

The Functional Approach

Parenthetically, while these leaders and older and more thoughtful union members necessarily at this time are primarily concerned with the utilitarian aspects of workers' education, they have not forgotten the importance of filling the worker's free time with constructive intellectual and cultural interests. Some American educators have made the ill-advised criticism that workers' education in this country is not as broadly cultural as, for example, the program of the British Workers' Educational Association. These educators will have to realize that the American tradition is different from the British tradition and that American labor history is replete with unsuccessful attempts of intellectuals to superimpose a cultural veneer upon the necessarily raw utilitarianism of American workers' education. More intellectual and cultural interests will be served when, as he will, the American worker discovers that he needs them.

The major problem facing effective college and university workers' education is in attempting to clarify and change some of the concepts and ideas of those who wish to replace workers' education with labor-management education.

Labor-management education starts on the assumption that labor and management today are on equal terms in strength and general acceptance. All that is lacking is the chance for both parties to sit around the table in the calm atmosphere of the classroom. Here the two parties will come to understand each other's problems and points of view, and stable industrial relations automatically will follow.

Workers' education calls this putting the cart before the horse. Labor does want stable industrial relations, but workers' education believes that it can arrive at the goal by a better route. That route lies along the road of satisfaction, first, of labor's primary and immediate internal needs, needs which may seem to have no direct bearing on industrial relations but which, in the long run, affect them greatly.

Labor-management education works on the premise that labor and management do not understand one another and that, therefore, they must be brought together.

Workers' education says that actually labor and management understand each other very well. Labor knows that management wants low costs and high profits. Management knows that labor wants higher wages and shorter hours. Slowly and painfully the two parties are learning to narrow the areas of conflict across which they face each other. Working separately with the help of educational specialists, the two parties, in homogeneous surroundings, can increase their understanding of the basic social and economic principles about which conflict swirls.

Ernest Schwarztrauber sharpens these differences and spells out the university's role in helping narrow areas of conflict between labor and management. Writing of the evolving labor-management relationship, he says:

> No one familiar with that evolution can but recognize that the conflicts incident to it have been between groups unequal in economic resources, in state and national legislative and judicial support, and all too often in the command of trained, well-equipped leadership, particularly in the field of technical labor, legal knowledge and the like.
>
> The speed of further modifications in conflicts will be determined, so far as organized labor is concerned, by all those processes that raise it to some degree of equality in bargaining with management.
>
> In terms of economic resources it probably cannot hope to equal that of capital nor would this necessarily be desirable.
>
> But in development of a unionism increasingly strengthened by the statesmanship of its leaders and the intelligence and alertness of its membership, labor can hope to arrive at equality with capital. And equality between the two will then narrow still further areas of conflict.
>
> The function of the university in the present status of industrial relations is, in my humble opinion, to give organized labor educational facilities whereby it can satisfy those internal needs that will help build it to some degree of equality with industry.
>
> The "understanding," and the "learning to know one another" that we hope to see between labor and management will then arise not in class room contacts but around the conference table in contract negotiations. And there too will take place the ironing out of conflicting interests.[3]

There is nothing in this functional approach to workers' education to which management and its supporters should object. It accepts the enterprise system. It attempts to help labor prepare more intelligently for negotiations with management on the successful com-

3. Ernest Schwarztrauber, *"The Wisconsin Idea"* in *Workers' Education, op. cit.*, pp. 6–7.

pletion of which, in large part, the preservation of that system depends. It attempts to assist labor to attain broader understanding of the economic, political and social problems facing the larger community of which both labor and management are important parts and to the solution of which both labor and management must contribute.

Discouraging past experiences with colleges and universities, particularly the University of Michigan fiasco, have convinced some labor leaders, and the workers' education specialists employed by them, that a functional approach to college and university workers' education is unattainable and that unions will have to finance and conduct all workers' education activities themselves. Many of their brothers and sisters who take a more optimistic view of the future of college and university workers' education feel that attainment of the functional approach on a large scale, although it is a long way off, is still possible. Survey and experience indicate that the latter probably are right.

If they are right, much of the blame for the situation must be accorded to labor itself. While theoretically unions are committed to agitate strongly for a fairer distribution of educational services, in practice this agitation is limited to occasional utterances from labor leaders to claims on the services of colleges and universities. It follows that it is unjust for intellectuals within the labor movement to condemn institutions of higher learning as hopelessly indifferent to workers' needs. They argue, or are sometimes tempted to argue, for their own system of workers' education on the false premise that the battle for honest public education in the United States is already lost. In actual fact, it has never really begun on the workers' education front. If these intellectuals saw to it that labor consistently maintained pressure for fair treatment, much could be achieved.

Aside from this lethargical attitude, some labor intellectuals are underestimating the real interests of their rank and file. It is doubtful that the worker prefers an isolated culture of his own to the general culture of the community. As T. R. Adam says, "It is doubtful if he would be satisfied with a specialized workers' culture, any more than he would be content with a grimly uniform workers' automobile."[4]

Yet to dissipate this union suspicion of university motivation will not be an easy task. Union leadership traditionally has been dis-

4. Adam, *op. cit.*, p. 7.

trustful of outside ideas and outside intellectuals. Union membership is not always accustomed to broadminded, vitally enlightening discussion of union and social problems within union halls — in fact, labor leaders who provide it often are suspected of seeking publicity. Workers' education, even in the labor movement, has never been fully accepted; therefore, it has always stepped lightly, never trying seriously to make either dangerous enemies or serious friends, and lacking purpose and plan. In view of this situation, it is not at all strange that professional educators within the labor movement should move very slowly in establishing firmer relationships with institutions of higher education about whose approach to workers' education they have serious reservations.

Kermit Eby and Frank Fernbach, men with long experience in workers' education, point up this fact:

> Educators must understand the deep-rooted suspicions of many wage earners. It must be remembered that organized labor has been forced, in many cases, to fight for existence in hostile communities where school boards and educators reflected the antagonisms of business groups. Some unionists may be hard to convince that even institutions of higher learning are objective in their teaching. College faculties must face skeptical worker students with tolerance and good nature, while they establish confidence that their instruction is not just subtle "propaganda" from management's point of view.[5]

While professors will do well to listen to Eby and Fernbach, labor leaders, in turn, will do well to listen to the acutely observant James Bryce, who once called German universities popular but not free, English universities free but not popular, and American universities both free and popular.[6] American colleges and universities have great potentiality in the field of workers' education; it is incumbent upon labor leaders to explore that potentiality by consistently agitating for the functional approach to it.

If all labor leaders took the position of Dr. Mollie Ray Carroll at a 1937 workers' education conference, there would be little difficulty. She stated that organized labor would be critical of college and university workers' education but that union suspicion would be "the critical attitude of people who care terribly about having it done

5. Eby and Fernbach, *op. cit.*, pp. 495–96.
6. Creese, *op. cit.*, p. 5.

The Functional Approach

well."[7] Unfortunately, the attitude of far too many union leaders, as Marius Hansome says, more closely parallels the tale of the Five Blind Men and the Elephant. Each is blind to everything except that which he wishes most.[8] Unless institutions of higher learning are willing to restrict themselves to the particular trade union policy and program of the moment, these labor leaders look upon them as pliable tools of reaction.

Part of this attitude is due to the fact that unions have little understanding of the nature and methods of colleges and universities. The university presents a paradox in that it is authoritarian in some respects and almost laissez faire in others. Labor does not understand this paradox.

Often top university administrations are not at all democratic. Labor finds that they cannot adapt themselves to union insistence on participation in the planning and organization of workers' education programs and in the classroom.

But universities also are loosely organized. There frequently is autonomy of departments and independence on the part of individual faculty members. Universities are devoted to the scientific method and give harbor and scope to people of widely different views. Labor finds little consistency that can be compared, for example, with the policy and program of the AFL and CIO. Labor sometimes therefore concludes that universities are aimless institutions which cannot make up their minds or take positions on issues.

Labor will have to realize that it is *not* the function of colleges and universities *as institutions* to decide whether union or industrial leaders are right or wrong on this or that specific issue or series of related issues. Labor must understand that it *is* the function of institutions of higher learning, after consultation with labor leaders and the workers' education specialists employed by them, to decide what felt needs, interests and problems of union officers and members they can help satisfy, answer and solve. This is the functional approach to college and university workers' education; it should be acceptable enough to organized labor to warrant consistent agitation in its behalf.

Any college or university which undertakes a workers' education

---

7. *Proceedings of the Twenty-Second Annual Convention of the National University Extension Association, op. cit.*, p. 61.
8. Hansome, *op. cit.*, p. 493.

program must accept this necessity for emphasis upon the immediate and internal problems of labor. This primary concern must be based upon certain beliefs and convictions. Frederick B. Harbison of the University of Chicago puts it this way:

> The basis for a Labor Education Program is the belief that a strong well led union is an essential part of the democratic process and that the American way of life as we know it cannot survive without the agency of the trade union. The betterment of industrial relations as such is only part of the objective of a sound Labor Education Program.
>
> This objective of helping to build strong unions can be implemented through the extension of the facilities of the College or University to the labor movement to train union technicians of all kinds, to provide special programs to various labor groups, to stimulate better thinking on the part of labor unions, to get the leaders of labor unions to see and think about their own problems, and to develop a realization on the part of labor leaders of the impact of union policies on the general public.
>
> The Universities with well equipped extension divisions are the ones to do the job.[9]

Any college or university which undertakes a program of workers' education will have to proceed on certain specific premises. First, it will have to view the trade union as an accepted institution in modern American industrial society, despite threatening situations which at times face it. Both legally and practically, the trade union has been woven into the fabric of American institutional life. Second, it will have to assert that collective bargaining, with full and equal participation on the part of the trade union, is the normal relationship between American employers and employees. Third, it will have to look at all labor as having essential dignity so long as it serves human welfare, and it will have to help labor develop a new creative pride in the work it performs. Fourth, it will have to plan and work in terms of long range as well as immediate worker needs. Workers are no longer mere hewers of stone and carriers of water; they are asserting their right and their desire to assume responsibility in the whole field of community life.

In practical operational terms this all means that the university

---

9. Quoted in Arthur, *op. cit.*, p. 10.

The Functional Approach

must realize that it cannot superimpose on workers' education programs whatever it considers good for workers; workers are adults and will have to be considered as such. The university therefore must begin its program where workers are, not where it might think workers ought to be. What workers consider to be their needs must be the basis for initial university service to them. The university's failure to see this latter point has been at the root of many a misunderstanding between institutions of higher learning and labor, particularly where a university has as its primary objective the dissemination of labor-management education. Workers cannot be expected to develop an appreciation of the problems of management when they are faced with a multiplicity of problems of their own awaiting solution.

Our survey shows that today only seven colleges and universities conducting workers' education frankly subscribe to a philosophical statement of function oriented toward satisfaction first of labor's immediate and internal problems. Over half of the institutions which currently have workers' education programs choose rather to be identified with a statement of function which holds that the underlying assumption of a workers' education program is that such specialized training will contribute directly to the achievement of better industrial relations. While ultimately both positions lead into the same end, there is a present important difference, which is that those institutions which take the former position are willing to put first things first — to function in terms of student needs and interests.

If all college and university extension division directors viewed workers' education as does L. H. Adolfson, Director of Extension, University of Wisconsin, and if reasons for beliefs such as his were clearly and completely explained to community groups, colleges and universities would find much of the present ignorance of and opposition to the purposes of workers' education dispelled. Adolfson says:

> To be effective, the teaching must recognize the philosophy of the American labor movement, and its approach to collective bargaining which it has always conceived as its paramount interest. Therefore, whatever the personal views of the teacher, he will naturally take cognizance in his teaching of the crystallized philosophy and objectives of the American labor movement. This philosophy of the American labor movement is grounded in faith in democracy and free enterprise and its ob-

jective is the improvement of the position of the workers within that basic framework, largely through the process of collective bargaining.[10]

Leaders of labor and management, and administrators of institutions of higher learning who have faith in democracy share a belief in the enterprise system, a belief in the collective bargaining process as an essential prop of that system, and a belief that increased understanding of the economic, social and political problems facing the larger community is imperative in these troubled times. They therefore should be willing to share a belief in the functional approach to workers' education, an approach which is rooted in the enterprise system and which attempts to increase understanding of both collective bargaining and larger community problems.

10. *Proceedings of the Thirty-Fourth Annual Meeting of the National University Extension Association, op. cit.*, p. 85.

8

Essentials of an Effective Functional College and University Workers' Education Program

INSTITUTIONS OF HIGHER learning which accept the functional approach to workers' education view their work with labor groups as the fruit of a cooperative union-university partnership in education, and have agreed to certain conditions of partnership.

Labor often asks: Can workers' education, when financed from non-labor sources, be guarded from dilution into something innocuous and sterile? And higher education turns this question around and asks: Can workers' education, when entirely labor's operation, escape the atrophy and narrowness which so often is the result of inbreeding? The unions and universities which accept the functional approach have answered these questions to each other's satisfaction.

They have come to the conclusion that the twin dangers of dilution and bias can be avoided if the possibility of their presence in both university-conducted and labor-conducted workers' education is recognized. They agree that, once this possibility is recognized, administrative safeguards can be devised against both dangers.

Ernest Schwarztrauber states that democratic representation in workers' education policy-making, an informed citizenry, and capable direction can provide positive administrative safeguards against biased or poor administration of workers' education programs.[1] Survey and experience support his statement.

State-financed programs must give workers a definite voice in policy-making. Labor people should have seats both on boards of trustees of colleges and universities and on advisory councils to workers' education programs conducted by universities. Labor and the university concerned should agree on such trustee and advisory council representatives. Faculty and students in the workers' education division should be consulted and invited to participate in policy-making, contributing out of their experience and desires to what finally might be decided. Labor-financed programs must give democratically selected representatives of the rank and file a voice in the administration of programs.

Reference to an informed citizenry is equally applicable to college and university and union-financed and controlled workers' education. The public must become aware of the fact that workers' education has a legitimate claim for public support, then no legislative disruption of workers' education as occurred at Wisconsin and no termination as occurred at Michigan will be possible on the flimsy grounds advanced in those two situations. Union members must be awakened to the necessity for an education department; they must learn to defend that department against attack from both within and without as long as it is helping them to meet their needs and solve their problems.

It follows that capable directors of workers' education, both in institutions of higher learning and in union education departments, are essential. They will have to be people with poise and balance in judgment, capacity to work democratically, knowledge of both the labor movement and the worker's language, and knowledge of both the purposes and techniques of workers' education.

Neither organized labor nor our colleges and universities singlehandedly can launch adequate programs of workers' education. The

---

1. Ernest Schwarztrauber, "Administering Workers' Education," *op. cit.*, pp. 227–29.

former lacks both resources and the requisite educational experience. The latter are without an adequate means of gaining understanding of the true needs of organized and unorganized workers.

Today workers' education is in much the same position as elementary education a hundred and twenty years ago. Organized labor then sought educational facilities for its children and finally turned to the public treasury. Organized labor today is seeking adequate educational facilities for its adult membership: it will have to turn again to the public treasury. Labor sooner or later will come to the conclusion that it would be foolish to accept educational instruments below the standard of public universities when it has a right to a fair share of the services of such tax supported institutions — sooner or later it will see that it has neither the financial resources nor sufficient trained personnel to educate its own people as labor extremists would have it do. Trends indicate that Paul Essert is right when he concludes that:

> Many universities and colleges will for a time resist labor control of the workers' education program, but probably there will be concessions by both organized labor and the universities in this respect. The point is that labor needs the university to help give the proper status and to develop a national group of labor educators, and the universities will increasingly recognize their responsibility to serve industrial labor as well as industrial management and agriculture.[2]

Unless these concessions come, we shall find ourselves looking at a workers' education movement which defines education as power over rather than as power with. We will have arrived at the admission that both sides to the argument have exhausted their intelligence and their good will and have decided that one or the other must be annihilated.

The best safeguards against such an impasse are competent workers' education administrators and teachers, both within and without the labor movement. They will be people with real knowledge of the labor movement and with sympathy for the aspirations of that movement not only for itself but for the entire community.

At a conference on workers' education held at Cornell University in February, 1946, the following qualifications, listed in the order

2. Essert, *op. cit.*, p. 10.

of their importance, were accepted as essential for university people responsible for a program of workers' education:

1. Union experience of such nature as to demonstrate sympathy for the social ideals of the labor movement and a knowledge of the structure and functioning of the labor movement.
2. Participation in some form of workers' education activities, especially in program development and, if possible, administration.
3. A record of success in group activity, including ability to cooperate with others.
4. Knowledge of the field of workers' education.
5. Knowledge of and ability in group work and educational processes as applied to workers' education.
6. Knowledge of and experience with community organizations and governmental agencies as related to their helpfulness as resources in a workers' education program.
7. Acceptability to people of known reputation in the field of workers' education.[3]

The workers' education teacher has been an important concern of colleges and universities for a long time. As early as 1924, one observer, studying the feasibility of expansion of college and university workers' education, stated that, "securing instructors would be one of the most serious matters and most of the men on our faculties would be entirely unsuited to the work."[4]

Even the best of university professors retain a methodology and a mental habit more traditionally acceptable in the undergraduate classroom. They are not prepared to deal with adults, particularly adult workers.

Thus, college and university workers' education programs have depended upon part-time services of specialists from within the labor movement, government, public schools, law and other areas for their teaching. The two principal qualifications presently used in selection of part-time instructors, experience in teaching adults and functional knowledge of the labor movement, will have to be adopted by all college and university programs which wish to employ

---

3. Orlie Pell, "Jobs in Workers' Education," *Adult Education Journal*, 9:68, April, 1950.
4. Norman C. Miller, "Report of Study for the National University Extension Association on the Matter of Cooperation Between State Institutions and Trade Union Bodies," *op. cit.*, p. 7.

teachers acceptable to the labor movement. More institutions of higher learning will have to take the position of J. O. Keller of Penn State who told the National University Extension Association that his institution is careful to select teachers who are either workers or professors who know and who have worked with the labor movement.[5]

Current college and university workers' education programs most acceptable to the labor movement are those which use labor people on their teaching staffs. Programs which use fully qualified teachers who happen to be employed full-time in the labor movement give tangible evidence of their belief that a class leader ought to be genuinely and fundamentally sympathetic with the problems and interests of the people in his class.

The good workers' education teacher faces a dual responsibility! He is responsible to the worker and to society as a whole. The first responsibility demands qualifications which persons employed in the labor movement, for obvious reasons, most adequately can present. The second is a general responsibility which all qualified teachers can satisfy and which links the workers' education teacher to all true teachers in every field.

Unions must avoid the tendency to conclude that the only good teachers are those who have grown up within the ranks of labor. To argue that one cannot be a teacher of workers unless he has been a worker is to argue that one cannot teach banking unless he has been a banker. If unions were to apply this qualification and were to reject all except those teachers trained only in the school of hard knocks, their educational activities would suffer greatly. There are not enough such teachers to go around.

Besides, the teacher drawn from labor's ranks very frequently lacks broad educational background. Although he is well acquainted with labor's immediate problems and needs, he has at hand neither the teaching techniques nor the broad knowledge of economics, political science and sociology necessary to drive home his material in the total context of modern society.

Ernest Schwarztrauber admirably describes the ideal workers' education teacher:

---

5. *Proceedings of the Twenty-Eighth Annual Meeting of the National University Extension Association at the Hotel Morrison, Chicago, Illinois, May 11–13, 1943* (Bloomington, Indiana: Feltus Printing Company, Inc., 1943), p. 32.

The teacher's function in a class of workers is that of guide and friendly cooperator in encouragement of discussion of specific problems. Those before him are adults, many with considerable experience as shop stewards, union officers and organizers. They possess a wealth of experience in industry. It is a teacher's skill which draws out in discussion that experience and makes it available to fellow students — and teacher. The teacher must be ready at all times to introduce his experience and his study for the benefit of the class. He is not a mere parliamentarian or chairman of a talk-fest. He directs and guides discussion along fruitful lines, as logical as possible in sequence. Hence, he must thoroughly plan each meeting with his group, deciding where he contributes and where the students themselves make their contributions. All this requires a skill which no traditional college or high school teacher knows or uses.[6]

Competent workers' education teachers realize that their function demands cooperative endeavor. Students as well as teachers contribute to problem-solving and need-satisfaction. Similar cooperative endeavor can be observed throughout the effective college and university workers' education program. It is a fourth essential for success.

Only if higher education and organized labor work together can we have effective college and university workers' education. The former brings to the common task professional skill, and the latter, knowledge of the needs and problems of workers. Their past and present experience with cooperative planning indicates that certain conditions must prevail.

First, the subject matter taught must be related to the actual experiences of workers in a particular group. If a basic collective bargaining class is conducted for a specific union, grievances discussed in class must be culled from the experience of the students and handled within the framework of the contract under which those grievances must be negotiated. If a one-day institute on Labor and Community Relations is conducted for a group of unions within a certain geographic area, topics chosen should be within the experiences of those who will participate, and speakers and resource people

---

6. Ernest E. Schwarztrauber, *The University of Wisconsin School for Workers: Its First Twenty-Five Years* (Madison, Wisconsin: University of Wisconsin School for Workers, 1946), p. 26.

Essentials of an Effective Program 137

should be thoroughly familiar with the needs and problems likely to be discussed under the topics chosen.

Second, instruction should be aimed at functional groups with common problems and interests. On the theory that people learn best when they are an homogeneous group studying common problems in a congenial atmosphere, college and university workers' education programs should gear their work to the many specialized groups in the average local union. Perhaps the education committee needs a short-term course in methods of handling audio-visual materials. Perhaps the stewards' council wants a series of discussions on arbitration for its next two or three meetings. Perhaps the general membership is confused as to the provisions of the amended workmen's compensation bill just passed by the state legislature, and would benefit from the opportunity to hear them explained by an expert who is also a skilled adult educator. This kind of specialized service tailored to the needs of particular groups within unions is what labor wants colleges and universities to provide.

Third, unions ask that college and university workers' education programs consult with them on the choice of topics, materials and speakers for the educational activities they conduct in cooperation with those programs.

Specifically, labor asks a willingness on the part of the college or university, before a collective bargaining class is scheduled, to discuss the particular needs and problems of the group for which the class is to be given. It also wants planning committees on which both union and university people serve when a Labor and the Community conference is in the making.

Fourth, all instruction should be based upon real problems of real workers. How can unions build up attendance at regular meetings, what practical psychological principles can unions use to imbue stewards with the seriousness of the job they must perform, how can a union handle an intercultural problem, how can the union help a widowed worker place her child in a nursery school? It is with practical problems such as these that unions are concerned, and it is on these practical problems that unions seek the assistance of college and university workers' education programs. Concern with theory in the various social sciences and with the broader cultural world handled so well by the British Workers Educational Association, the kinds of educational activity which most colleges and universities would like workers to consider, will come later as the American labor movement grows and evolves and as it begins to feel the need for them.

Effective programs, those on which university and union can agree, will stress wholehearted participation by students in discussions of problems they face. Study will be conducted in a democratic atmosphere, with the teacher a member of the group, and full consideration will be given to the experiences of the students. Students will be assisted in thinking over and testing their ideas, in gathering facts, in developing skills and techniques. Their study will result in enthusiasm for the cause of labor and for their own participation in that cause.

Mechanics of programming is another problem which must be given greater consideration. Mechanics usually are either passed over or left on the "you-will-know-what-to-do" basis when programs are being discussed between union and university.

There are several aspects of the mechanics of programming which deserve serious thought by both union and university.

There is the question of length of courses and other educational activity. Current college and university practice emphasizes short-term courses; most institutions run classes aggregating twelve or fewer sessions, with the majority favoring courses holding between six and ten meetings. This practice is approved by the labor movement and is the rule with labor-conducted workers' education classes. The reasons for it are easy to understand. Workers want subject matter that is practical in character and specific by nature, and stewards would like in as short as possible a time to learn how to write and negotiate a grievance. Workers most often attend classes on their own time after they have put in eight hours on the job. Experience has shown that they are reluctant to give up certain hours on certain days except for short periods of time.

One-day regional institutes, preferably on a Saturday, are most popular with workers. Longer sessions involving either lost-time from the job or the giving up of family claims on Sunday can be conducted occasionally; they cannot be overdone.

Summer school sessions are considered most productive when conducted for a week and when they combine opportunities for education with the opportunity for a vacation. In some instances, provision of facilities for wives who may wish to come along are very helpful in building both interest and attendance.

Equally important is the length of single course sessions and the various instructional periods at regional institutes and summer schools. Current practice favors course sessions two hours in length and institute and summer school instructional periods of about the same duration. Two hours is long enough for rather full discussion of one or several specific topics and yet not so long as to become tedious when properly handled.

Thorough attention should be given to the physical aspects of the meeting place. Smoking should be allowed, and provision made for comfortable seating which affords the opportunity for taking notes, as well as a seating arrangement conducive to discussion. Adequate lighting and ventilation and easy access to toilet and drinking facilities are also essential.

Workers who give of their own time and effort to participate in educational activities should receive some kind of overt recognition of the fact. Certificates of attendance should be given to those who complete courses, and perhaps diplomas in basic leadership training for those who complete a series of courses designed to provide such training. These certificates and diplomas should be presented at regular union meetings, with a representative of the college or university on hand to assist in the presentation. This practice already is observed by some programs and meets with approval in almost every quarter of the labor movement.

Joint planning of program is traditional and accepted in university extension, the university division through which most college and university workers' education programs operate.

Labor points to the existence of cooperation with business and farm groups and with technical and professional societies as precedent for the establishment or expansion of joint planning of activities by college and university workers' education programs.

Such planning is essential to a successful college and university workers' education program and institutions of higher learning will have to give more than lip service to the principle. If union education directors are unanimous on any one point, this is it. Without provision for labor participation in program planning, college and university workers' education programs will find themselves either severely handicapped or totally unable to continue operations on any appreciable scale with bona fide labor groups. John D. Connors says, "It is of first importance that the plan of the program and the working out of its details should be the joint effort of representatives both of labor and the university."[7]

Methods of cooperation between various colleges and universities and the labor movement now differ considerably and will continue to differ. However, as our survey shows, many institutions of higher learning in the field accept in practice the principle of consultation and joint planning, and do not attempt to hand out workers' education on a "take it or leave it" basis. Experienced colleges and universities have learned that only as they are willing to discover what the educational needs and interests of labor groups are can they hope to meet them adequately.

Joint planning does not mean that colleges and universities are turning over the responsibility for content and method to labor any more than they turn it over to any other group seeking specialized service. Nor does it mean that the university limits itself to providing housekeeping facilities for union-controlled and conducted workers' education programs.

It does mean that widespread suspicion of university attitudes toward labor can be dispelled by performance and not by protestation. Where union and university sit down together to plan programs for workers, an atmosphere of mutual trust can be developed and a functional partnership in education evolved. This possibility was discovered by some university administrators as long ago as 1925. It is unfortunate that more colleges and universities have not been as willing to experiment as has California.

> The Extension Division of the University of California has had the experience of serving labor organizations when the control was vested in the University alone and later when this service was under the direction of an advisory committee, a majority of whose members were drawn from the State Federation of Labor. As was to be expected, there has been little or no change in the demands for training and instruction.[8]

7. John D. Connors, *How to Set Up a Labor Institute, op. cit.*, p. 2.
8. *Proceedings of the National University Extension Association at Charlottesville, Virginia, April 30, May 1, 2, 1925* (Boston: Wright and Potter Printing Company, 1925), p. 43.

Essentials of an Effective Program 141

But with labor participation, there was a clearer and more definite idea of the needs and problems of the workers who were to be served. Labor groups could be guided toward discovery and articulation of their needs, and programs could be based upon those needs.

Colleges and universities today are becoming more interested in the broader field of labor-management education as well as in that of workers' education. The stated basis of their interest in the former field is development of improved industrial relations. But how can a college or university "sell" genuine cooperation between labor and management unless it functions cooperatively in the planning, development and presentation of its services to workers?

Union education directors and realistic college and university workers' education program administrators realize that there can be no compromise on this principle of joint consultation and planning. It is an indispensable essential for assuring the success of college and university workers' education programs.

Closely related to cooperative development of programs is the need for maintenance of full liaison between college and university workers' education programs and the labor movement.

Such liaison must be based upon mutual understanding and respect. Colleges and universities which conduct workers' education programs will have to have a thorough grounding in the background and development of the labor movement. There should be people on their workers' education program staffs who have had experience in the trade union field. Institutions with programs should make every effort to keep up with developments in labor-conducted workers' education. George Guernsey says that colleges and universities interested in workers' education should know and understand various union departments, visit union educational conferences and summer schools, and familiarize themselves with what labor is doing with audio-visual media. Guernsey's statement has been seconded by the AFL's John D. Connors and by educational specialists employed by international unions affiliated with both national federations of labor.

Since the development of understanding is a two-way process, labor leaders and labor educators will have to make earnest efforts to understand what we have called the paradox of the university. They will have to learn why a university harbors men of various shades of economic and political opinion ranging from extreme left to extreme right. By insisting on the use of the consultative function and joint planning they can help make the higher echelons of university administration less autocratic and more responsive to the ideas and criticisms of those they exist to serve and those who serve under them.

We live in a time of urgent crisis. We are part of a radically changing world. The acknowledged first task of modern education is to assist us to shed the dead stocks of ideas that have been suited to other times and older institutions but which now block the path that lies ahead. The second task of modern education follows from this. It is to develop new standards of thinking that take their energy from present-day institutional life as it is shaped by constantly occurring social, political and economic changes and interests.

The university has always tried to extend the frontiers of knowledge. The modern labor movement is one of our strongest bulwarks against totalitarianism and stands with the university at the frontier of expanding democracy. Close liaison on workers' education programs thus is one aspect of the broader problem facing the university, labor, and the whole of society.

This one aspect is being handled fairly well by colleges and universities now in the field of workers' education. A majority of them consult with labor both on over-all program and direction and on specific local programs. However, college and university workers' education programs would benefit greatly from more discussion as to technique.

Evaluation procedures, an important part of liaison maintenance, should be more specific and less superficial than they now are. There presently is far too great a tendency to ignore the instructor and students at evaluation time—too much is left to the university workers' education administrator and the union scheduling officer who, at best, are present for only a minimum of class or discussion sessions.

Certain definite essentials for evaluation should be given more attention. Outside adult education specialists should be called in periodically to evaluate specific projects. Further thought is needed on measures used in evaluative procedure. When objectives are analyzed, are intermediate and long range as well as immediate objectives examined? When efficiency is assessed, are all aspects of administrative and teaching staff functions considered? Are physical arrangements and mechanics of scheduling given attention? Are teaching methods analyzed?

Essentials of an Effective Program

Is full use made of the many evaluative techniques available today? Most current programs ask participants to evaluate various kinds of activities they have scheduled. Many of them supplement these interviews with questionnaires, often filled out both by teacher and student. However, few programs make use of process and content observers, control groups, rating scales prepared by outside experts, and evaluating committees on which both union and university personnel serve.

Evaluation is perhaps the weakest area in workers' education today. Possible standards should be examined, decisions made as to those which are best, and then the standards selected should be applied by union and university working together as part of developing liaison.

While most college and university workers' education programs report that they do inform union education departments of the work they do with local affiliates, only two report quarterly, four semiannually and six annually. A majority of the institutions report at unspecified times.

It is essential that union education departments know what is going on educationally within the union at any given time of the year. Every such department is both over-worked and under-staffed and needs full cooperation from colleges and universities conducting classes or other educational activities for affiliates of the union. Unless union education directors know what is being done and what local problems and needs are, they cannot plan intelligently at the national level.

College and university workers' education programs which report both the problems and the needs which they discover in consultations with local people are making a major contribution to the liaison process. By keeping lines of communication open between union education officers and themselves, they make possible a wider and more effective dissemination of educational resources available both from within and without the labor movement.

Establishment of uniform procedures for obtaining this liaison is needed to accomplish central gathering of information on all current workers' education activities.

If all college and university workers' education programs will begin to send monthly reports to international union directors of education, summarizing discovered educational needs and problems of affiliated local unions and describing the steps being taken to help satisfy and solve them, liaison can get under way. These directors could then make reports to AFL and CIO education departments who could work out a final summary which could then be routed back to both union and university workers' education specialists. Included in this final summary would be, of course, the work being conducted within the labor movement itself.

Cooperation and liaison between college and university and union workers' education are key essentials which must be accepted by both if a vital and extensive workers' education movement within institutions of higher learning is to develop to the stage which demand indicates as attainable. Once there is functional agreement, procedures on over-all philosophy and on specifics such as subject matter, teaching personnel, methods and mechanics can be decided through negotiation.

Obligations of labor leaders and union members have multiplied many times over during the past two decades. What organized labor does or fails to do today may well decide the nature of tomorrow. Organized labor is one of the few bulwarks, and perhaps strongest of the few, against a violent dropping of the iron curtain on modern civilization. It emphasizes the dignity of the human personality and the lifting of the common man to new and higher levels of attainment and well-being. Workers' education is the medium it uses to point up its beliefs.

Alert American labor realizes that its educational programs eventually must be as broad as the best offered by general education.

A broadly educated American labor movement is an essential social institution in a time when democracy and totalitarianism are struggling for control of the world. It is the guarantee that an autocratic industrial state will not come into being within the framework of a democratic political state. But labor vision and statesmanship do not automatically evolve **out of** the rough and tumble of the collective bargaining process.

What is required is the gathering and sifting of facts, reflection upon and critical analysis of those facts, the drawing up of blueprints for action on the basis of digestion of those facts and, finally, action itself. This is the process of general education. If labor is to utilize it, the labor movement must have access to every educational facility it can use to advantage.

Essentials of an Effective Program

Workers' education therefore must be of concern not only to workers but also to every American who believes in democracy. College and university workers' education has the responsibility of helping labor transcend the narrow limits of specialized skill training to reach larger economic, social and political problems. It is upon the solution of these problems that a constantly improving democratic way of life depends.

The functional approach to college and university workers' education can get at these problems because it is shot through with pioneering sense, willingness to experiment, and emphasis on practicality.

Workers' education itself is symptomatic of transition and social adventurousness. It is in a stage of exploration where its influence is greater than its handicaps and its struggle to expand. It arouses either violent controversy or ebullient enthusiasm wherever it is discussed in college and university circles.

Colleges and universities in workers' education will have to face the fact that the blood pressures of conservative business and industrial leaders, timid trustees and sheltered pedagogues will go up in direct ratio to the broadness of the program offered. To a broad workers' education program, controversies and violent arguments are indispensable appurtenances. Economic heresies are heatedly discussed, industry's motives and incentives are openly questioned, and serious proposals for social change made. Out of all this comes not merely the teaching of skills but broader and better understanding of social, political and economic problems facing democracy. Discussion of these things is a part of the role of a university in its community. As our colleges and universities expand and extend broad workers' education programs democracy will take on greater reality and new vitality.

Bibliography

BOOKS

Adam, T. R., *The Worker's Road to Learning.* New York: American Association for Adult Education, 1940. 162 pp.

Hansome, Marius, *World Workers' Educational Movements: Their Social Significance.* New York: Columbia University Press, 1931. 594 pp.

Price, T. W., *The Story of The Workers' Educational Association 1903–1924.* London: Labour Publishing Company Ltd., 1924. 94 pp.

Schneider, Florence H., *Patterns of Workers' Education: The Story of the Bryn Mawr Summer School.* Washington: American Council on Public Affairs, 1941. 158 pp.

Schwarztrauber, Ernest E., *Workers' Education: A Wisconsin Experiment.* Madison, Wisconsin: University of Wisconsin Press, 1942. 182 pp.

Ware, Caroline F., *Labor Education in Universities.* New York: American Labor Education Service, 1946. 138 pp.

PAMPHLETS

Cohn, Fannia M., *Why Workers' Education?* New York: International Ladies' Garment Workers Union Educational Department, 1948. 4 pp.

Connors, John D., *How to Set Up a Labor Institute.* New York: Workers Education Bureau of America, 1947. 5 pp.

———, *Workers' Education: What? Why? How?* New York: Workers Education Bureau of America, 1947. 19 pp.

Educational Classes in Your Local Union: A Joint Union-University Program. Pittsburgh: United Steelworkers of America, 1949. 8 pp.

Labor and Education in 1949. New York: American Federation of Labor, 1950. 43 pp.

Bibliography 147

Miller, Jr., Spencer, *The University and the American Worker.* New York: Workers Education Bureau of America, 1922. 19 pp.

Miller, Jr., Spencer and Ruth Taylor, *The Pioneer Institute of Labor: An Experiment in Understanding.* New York: The Workers Education Bureau of America, 1945. 40 pp.

Report and Recommendation, Commission of Inquiry on the Workers Educational Service of University of Michigan. Detroit: Michigan Committee on Civil Rights, 1949. 11 pp.

Ruskin College: What It Is and What It Stands For. London: Cooperative Printing Society, Ltd., 1918. 24 pp.

Schwarztrauber, Ernest E., *The University of Wisconsin School for Workers: Its First Twenty-Five Years.* Madison: University of Wisconsin School for Workers, 1949. 40 pp.

———, "The Wisconsin Idea" in Workers Education. Madison, Wisconsin: University of Wisconsin School for Workers, 1946. 19 pp.

Starr, Mark, *Workers' Education.* New York: International Ladies' Garment Workers Union, 1943. 2 pp.

———, *Workers' Education Today.* New York: League for Industrial Democracy, 1941. 48 pp.

PERIODICAL ARTICLES

Bell, Daniel, "The Worker and His Civic Functions." *Monthly Labor Review,* 71: 62–9, July, 1950.

Barta, Elizabeth, "Let People Know: Roosevelt's Labor Education Division is Nationally Unique," *The Blotter,* pp. 7–9, March, 1950.

Bradley, Phillips, "The University's Role in Workers' Education," *Adult Education Journal,* 8:81–90, April, 1949.

Brameld, Theodore, "Workers' Education in America," *Educational Administration and Supervision,* 33:129–40, March, 1947.

Brown, Leo Cyril, "Catholic-Sponsored Labor-Management Education," *Journal of Educational Sociology,* 30:510–12, April, 1947.

Carroll, Mollie Ray, "The Emergency Education Program and Labor," *Journal of Adult Education,* 6:493–98, October, 1934.

Cohn, Fannia M., "Philosophy of Workers' Education," *Industrial and Labor Relations Review,* 1:705–708, July, 1948.

Connors, John D., "A New Frontier: Workers' Education and the University," *Adult Education Journal,* 5:73–7, April, 1946.

Dunlop, John T. and James J. Healy, "The University's Contribution to Advanced Labor Education," *Journal of Educational Sociology,* 30:472–77, April, 1947.

Eby, Kermit and Frank Fernbach, "Unions Look at Education in Industrial Relations," *Journal of Educational Sociology,* 30:494–99, April, 1947.

Kerchen, John L., "California Plan Expanded on Pacific Coast," *Journal of Adult Education*, 6:521–25, October, 1934.

Kerrison, Irvine L. H., "Rutgers Serves New Jersey Labor," *Workers Education Bureau News Letter*, 12:7, June, 1950.

———, "Using Films and Stripfilms with Union Groups," *Film Forum Review*, 3:13–15, Winter, 1948–49.

Miller, Jr., Spencer, "Labor Institutes," *Journal of Adult Education*, 6:510–13, October, 1934.

———, "Retrospect and Forecast in Workers' Education," *Journal of Adult Education*, 8:345–46, June, 1936.

Pell, Orlie, "Jobs in Workers' Education," *Adult Education Journal*, 9:66–73, April, 1950.

Smith, Hilda W., "Federal Cooperation in the Education of Workers," *Journal of Adult Education*, 6:499–505, October, 1934.

———, "New Directions in Workers' Education," *Journal of Adult Education*, 12:165–66, April, 1940.

Starr, Mark, "Building and Defending Democracy: I. The Role of Workers' Education," *The Educational Forum*, 13:287–92, March, 1949.

———, "Unions Look at Education in Industrial Relations," *Journal of Educational Sociology*, 30:499–502, April, 1947.

"The University and Labor Education," *Monthly Labor Review*, 65:36–40, July, 1947.

"University Classes for Workers," *School and Society*, 48:330, September 10, 1938.

Ware, Caroline F., "Trends in University Programs for Labor Education," *Industrial and Labor Relations Review*, 3:54–69, October, 1949.

Woods, Baldwin M. and Abbott Kaplan, "Areas and Services of University Extension in Industrial-Relations Programs," *Journal of Educational Sociology*, 30:484–89, April, 1947.

ESSAYS

Coit, Eleanor G., "Workers' Education," *Handbook of Adult Education in the United States*. Mary L. Ely, editor; New York: Institute of Adult Education, 1948. Pp. 30–36.

Hochwalt, Frederick G., "Catholic Adult Educational Activity," *Handbook of Adult Education in the United States*. Mary L. Ely, editor; New York: Institute of Adult Education, 1948. Pp. 187–91.

Kaplan, Abbott, "Labor-Management Programs," *Handbook of Adult Education in the United States*. Mary L. Ely, editor; New York: Institute of Adult Education, 1948. Pp. 37–41.

GOVERNMENT DOCUMENTS

Labor Education Extension Service. Senate Document no. 72321, Eightieth Congress, Second Session. Washington: U. S. Government Printing Office, 1948. 304 pp.

Labor Extension Act of 1949. House Document No. 94822, Eighty-First Congress, First Session. Washington: U. S. Government Printing Office, 1949. 273 pp.

Senate Bill No. 110. Report No. 92, Calendar No. 76, Eighty-First Congress, First Session, introduced January 5, 1949. 14 pp.

PARTS OF SERIES

Dix, Lester, *Higher Education Services to Adult Education in New York State,* University of the State of New York Bulletin No. 1357. Albany: University of the State of New York, December 1, 1948. 38 pp.

Fernbach, Alfred P., *University Extension and Workers' Education.* Studies in University Extension Education, No. 3. Bloomington, Indiana: The National University Extension Association, 1945. 32 pp.

PUBLICATIONS OF LEARNED ORGANIZATIONS

Baker, Frank E., "Relations With Public Education: An Overview of the Issues," Workers' Education in the United States, pp. 230–48. *Fifth Yearbook of the John Dewey Society.* New York: Harper and Brothers Publishers, 1941. 338 pp.

Brameld, Theodore, "Toward a Philosophy of Workers' Education," Workers' Education in the United States, pp. 278–302. *Fifth Yearbook of the John Dewey Society.* New York: Harper and Brothers Publishers, 1941. 338 pp.

Counts, George S. and Theodore Brameld, "Relations With Public Education: Some Specific Issues and Proposals," Workers' Education in the United States, pp. 249–77. *Fifth Yearbook of the John Dewey Society.* New York: Harper and Brothers Publishers, 1941. 338 pp.

Hardman, J. B. S., "The Challenge and the Opportunity," Workers' Education in the United States, pp. 3–24. *Fifth Yearbook of the John Dewey Society.* New York: Harper and Brothers Publishers, 1941. 338 pp.

Proceedings of the Eighth Annual Conference National University Extension Association at St. Louis, Missouri, April 19, 20, 21, 1923. Boston: Wright and Potter Printing Company, 1923. 163 pp.

Proceedings of the National University Extension Association at

Austin, Texas, May 13, 14, 15, 1929. Bloomington: Indiana University Press, 1929. 192 pp.

Proceedings of the National University Extension Association at Chapel Hill, North Carolina, April 25, 26, 27, 1927. Boston: Wright and Potter Printing Company, 1927. 207 pp.

Proceedings of the National University Extension Association at Charlottesville, Virginia, April 30, May 1, 2, 1925. Boston: Wright and Potter Printing Company, 1925. 154 pp.

Proceedings of the National University Extension Association at Lawrence, Kansas, April 25, 26, 27, 1928. Indianapolis: Wm. B. Burford Printing Company, 1928. 220 pp.

Proceedings of the National University Extension Association at Lexington, Kentucky, April 20, 21, 22, 1922. Boston: Wright and Potter Printing Company, 1922. 174 pp.

Proceedings of the National University Extension Association at Madison, Wisconsin, May 8, 9, 10, 1924. Boston: Wright and Potter Printing Company, 1924. 201 pp.

Proceedings of the National University Extension Association at Salt Lake City, Utah, June 7, 8, 9, 10, 1926. Boston: Wright and Potter Printing Company, 1926. 176 pp.

Proceedings of the Twenty-First Annual Convention of the National University Extension Association at The Louisiana State University, Baton Rouge, Louisiana, May 7–9, 1936. Indianapolis: Wm. B. Burford Printing Company, 1936. 173 pp.

Proceedings of the Twenty-Second Annual Convention of the National University Extension Association at Washington University, St. Louis, Missouri, May 13–15, 1937. Spencer, Indiana: Samuel M. Guard and Co., Inc., Printers, 1937. 150 pp.

Proceedings of the Twenty-Fifth Annual Convention of the National University Extension Association at Ann Arbor, Michigan, May 15–18, 1940. Bloomington, Indiana: Feltus Printing Company, Inc., 1940. 247 pp.

Proceedings of the Twenty-Sixth Annual Convention of the National University Extension Association at Oklahoma City, Oklahoma, May 5–7, 1941. Bloomington, Indiana: Feltus Printing Company, Inc., 1941. 288 pp.

Proceedings of the Twenty-Eighth Annual Meeting of the National University Extension Association at The Hotel Morrison, Chicago, Illinois, May 11–13, 1943. Bloomington, Indiana: Feltus Printing Company, Inc., 1943. 101 pp.

Proceedings of the Twenty-Ninth Annual Meeting of the National University Extension Association at The Hotel Statler, St. Louis, Missouri, May 3 and 4, 1944. Bloomington, Indiana: Feltus Printing Company, Inc., 1944. 66 pp.

Bibliography

Proceedings of the Thirty-First Annual Meeting of the National University Extension Association at The Rockham Building, Detroit, Michigan, April 23 to 26, 1946. Bloomington, Indiana: Feltus Printing Company, Inc., 1946. 196 pp.

Proceedings of the Thirty-Second Annual Meeting of the National University Extension Association at The Hotel Dennis, Atlantic City, New Jersey, May 6, 7, 8 and 9, 1947. Bloomington, Indiana: Feltus Printing Company, Inc., 1947. 152 pp.

Proceedings of the Thirty-Third Annual Meeting of the National University Extension Association at The Hotel Shoreland, Chicago, Illinois, May 2–5, 1948. Bloomington, Indiana: Feltus Printing Company, Inc., 1948. 224 pp.

Proceedings of the Thirty-Fourth Annual Meeting of the National University Extension Association at Edgewater Gulf Hotel, Edgewater Park, Mississippi, May 2–5, 1949. Bloomington, Indiana: Feltus Printing Company, Inc., 1949. 160 pp.

Schwarztrauber, Ernest E., "Administering Workers' Education," Workers' Education in the United States, pp. 203–29. *Fifth Yearbook of the John Dewey Society*. New York: Harper and Brothers Publishers, 1941. 338 pp.

Smith, Hilda W., "The Student and Teacher in Workers' Education," Workers' Education in the United States, pp. 181–202. *Fifth Yearbook of the John Dewey Society*. New York: Harper and Brothers Publishers, 1941. 338 pp.

NEWSPAPERS

The Detroit Free Press, May 20, 1948 through March 23, 1949.
The Detroit News, May 20, 1948 through March 23, 1949.
The Detroit Times, May 21, 1948.
The Wage Earner (Detroit, Michigan), May 21, 1948.

UNPUBLISHED MATERIALS

Arthur, J. B. M., "Report of the Recorder: Industrial Relations and Workers' Education Section Meeting." Unpublished report section of meeting of National University Extension Association, Chicago, May 4–5, 1948. 16 pp.

Essert, Paul L., "Adult Education in the United States: A Report on General and Institutional Trends Based on an Extended Tour of the Nation in 1947–1948." Unpublished report to Teachers College, Columbia University, New York, 1948. 18 pp.

Guernsey, George T., "The Education Program of the National CIO: Possible Lines of Cooperation with Universities." Unpublished paper read before University–Labor Education Conference, U. S. Department of Labor, Washington, May 29, 1947. 7 pp.

Hallenbeck, Wilbur C., "Diagnosis of the Problem of Participation." Unpublished paper read before annual meeting of American Association for Adult Education, Cleveland, May 4, 1950. 6 pp.

"Industrial Relations Work of Certain Universities — I." Unpublished Industrial Relations Memo Number 101, Industrial Relations Counsellors, Inc., New York, July 30, 1948. 46 pp.

"Industrial Relations Work of Certain Universities — II." Unpublished Industrial Relations Memo Number 106, Industrial Relations Counsellors, Inc., New York, February 21, 1949. 51 pp.

"Industrial Relations Work of Certain Universities — III." Unpublished Industrial Relations Memo Number 110, Industrial Relations Counsellors, Inc., New York, July 15, 1949. 60 pp.

Luchek, Anthony, "Workers' Education in Three Universities." Unpublished paper, The Pennsylvania State College, State College, Pennsylvania, 1949. 16 pp.

Miller, Norman C., "Report of Study for the National University Extension Association on the Matter of Cooperation Between State Institutions and Trade Union Bodies together with a Series of Letters from Prominent Industrial and Business Leaders Dealing with the Subject." Unpublished report, 1924. 13 pp.

"Report of the Group Assigned to Study the Problem of 'How Adult Education Can Assist Organized Labor to Increase Participation of Its Members in Public Affairs.'" Unpublished report of meetings held during the twenty-fifth annual meeting of the American Association for Adult Education, Cleveland, May 4–6, 1950. 5 pp.

"Report on Workers' Education Standards Based on Study by Local 189, AFT–AFL." Unpublished report read before annual meeting of Local 189, New York, February, 1948. 13 pp.

Smith, Hilda W., "History of the Labor Extension Bill: 1942–1950." Unpublished report read before meeting of National Committee for the Extension of Labor Education, Washington, May 26, 1950. 7 pp.

"Suggestions to Universities in Workers' Education." Unpublished conclusions of university-labor conference conducted by Union Leadership Training Project, University of Chicago, Chicago, October 11–14, 1949. 12 pp.

Witte, Edwin F., "The University and Labor Education." Unpublished paper read before the University Labor Education Conference, Washington, May 28, 1947. 25 pp.

"Workers' Education." Unpublished report prepared by Special Committee of the National University Extension Association, Madison, Wisconsin, May 1924. 15 pp.

Bibliography

INTERVIEWS

The following persons were interviewed by the author during the period from March to December, 1950.

John Armstrong, Industrial Relations Collection Librarian, Harvard University, Cambridge, Mass.

John Baird, Extension Division, University of New Hampshire, Durham, N. H.

Ralph Campbell, Director of Extension, New York State School of Industrial and Labor Relations, Cornell University, Ithaca, N. Y.

W. Ellison Chalmers, Director, Institute of Labor and Industrial Relations, University of Illinois, Champaign, Illinois.

Myron H. Clark, Director, Labor-Management Institute, University of Connecticut, Storrs, Connecticut.

Milton Derber, Coordinator of Research, Institute of Labor and Industrial Relations, University of Illinois, Champaign, Illinois.

Dorothy Dowell, Editor, Institute of Labor and Industrial Relations, University of Illinois, Champaign, Illinois.

John T. Dunlop, Professor of Economics, Harvard University, Cambridge, Massachusetts.

Frederick G. Dunn, Supervisor, Workers Education, Rhode Island State College, Providence, R. I.

Eleanor Emerson, New York State School of Industrial and Labor Relations, Cornell University, Chicago, Ill.

Phillips Garman, Coordinator of Extension, Institute of Labor and Industrial Relations, University of Illinois, Champaign, Ill.

John J. Glynn, Field Representative, Labor–Management Institute, University of Connecticut, Storrs, Conn.

John R. Hackett, Director, Division of General College Extension, Rhode Island State College, Providence, R. I.

James J. Healy, Executive Director, Trade Union Fellowship Program, Harvard University, Cambridge, Mass.

John Hogan, Economics Department Head, University of New Hampshire, Durham, N. H.

A. A. Liveright, Director, Union Leadership Training Project, University of Chicago, Chicago, Ill.

Anthony Luchek, Head, Labor Education Service, Pennsylvania State College, State College, Pa.

Frank McAllister, Director, Labor Education Division, Roosevelt College, Chicago, Ill.

Ralph McCoy, Librarian, Institute of Labor and Industrial Relations, University of Illinois, Champaign, Ill.

George S. Paul, Executive Secretary, Labor–Management Institute, University of Connecticut, Storrs, Conn.

Effie Riley, Extension Division, New York State School of Labor and Industrial Relations, Cornell University, New York, N. Y.

Robert L. Stutz, Extension Manager, Labor–Management Institute, University of Connecticut, Storrs, Conn.

LETTERS

The following persons contributed information by letter during 1950.

F. H. Bird, Dean, College of Business Administration, University of Cincinnati.

J. Douglas Brown, Director, Industrial Relations Section, Princeton University.

Mary B. Clark, Executive Secretary, Labor and Management Center, Yale University.

Lewis Corey, Professor of Political Economy, Antioch College.

Edward L. Cushman, Director, Institute of Industrial Relations, Wayne University.

Carl T. Devine, School of Commerce, University of Southern California.

Henry J. Engler, Jr., Associate Professor of Management, Loyola University (New Orleans).

B. Felix Francis, Department of Economics, LaSalle College.

Rev. E. J. Hamel, St. Michael's College.

Ronald W. Haughton, Assistant Director, Institute of Industrial Relations, University of California.

I. O. Horsfall, Director, Extension Division, University of Utah.

Glenn S. Jensen, Administrative Assistant, Extension Division, University of Colorado.

Victor L. Jepsen, Associate Professor of Business Administration, Fresno State College.

Charles C. Killingsworth, Head, Department of Economics, Michigan State College.

Director, Labor Relations Institute, University of Puerto Rico.

Charles N. Lanier, Chairman, Department of Economics and Business Administration, University of Delaware.

C. H. Lawshe, Professor of Psychology, Purdue University.

J. J. MacAllister, Associate Director, Department of Institutional and Industrial Management, Mississippi State College.

Rev. E. C. McCue, Dean, John Carroll University.

Fred J. Meyer, Assistant to the Director, Bureau of Labor and Management, State University of Iowa.
J. R. Morton, Director, Continuation Education, University of Alabama.
Thomas E. Posey, Department of Economics, West Virginia State College.
Willis H. Reals, Dean, University College, Washington University.
C. K. Searles, Dean, College of Business Administration, University of Toledo.
Ronald B. Shuman, Professor of Business Management, University of Oklahoma.
E. J. Soop, Director, Extension Division, University of Michigan.
Lucille Speer, Documents and Serials Librarian, Montana State University.
Harold F. Sylvester, Professor of Personnel Administration, University of Maryland.
E. A. Tabler, Assistant Director of Adult Education, University of Akron.
Colston Warne, Professor of Economics, Amherst College.
Martha L. Wieners, Executive Secretary, Office of the Dean, Barnard College.
Rev. Henry J. Wirtenberger, Evening College of Commerce and Finance, University of Detroit.
Louis A. Wood, Professor Emeritus, University of Oregon.
George B. Zehmer, Director, Extension Division, University of Virginia.

Appendix I: Survey Questionnaire: Current Experiences of Colleges and Universities in Workers' Education

Administration
1. Name of college or university
2. Is college or university
   a. Public ....
      1.) State University ....
      2.) Land grant college ....
      3.) Municipal ....
   b. Private ....
      1.) Non sectarian ....
      2.) Religious ....
         a.) Catholic .... Order ....
         b.) Jewish ....
         c.) Protestant .... Denomination ....
3. Title of agency within college or university which conducts workers' education program
4. Name and title of person in charge of workers' education program
   a. Are you that person?
      Yes .... No ....
   b. If not, your name and title
5. Name and title of person to whom workers' education administrator responsible
6. Does workers' education administrator have tenure?
   Yes .... No ....

Appendix I 157

7. Check *each* area in which workers' education administrator has background. Check area in which he has *major* background

        Background   *Major* Background
  a. Government ....
  b. Labor   ....
  c. Management ....
  d. University   ....

Aids to Administration

8. Has your workers' education program a *lay* advisory committee?
        Yes ....   No ....
  a. This committee has ....(number) members
  b. They come from
                (number)
    1.) Government ....
    2.) Labor   ....
    3.) Management ....
    4.) Public   ....
  c. Members of this committee are
    1.) Appointed .... By whom ....
        Term ....
    2.) Elected   .... By whom ....
        Term ....
  d. This committee meets
    1.) Quarterly   ....
    2.) Semiannually ....
    3.) Annually   ....
    4.) Other stated intervals *(describe)*
  e. This committee has a *stated* function?
    1.) Yes *(describe)* .... 2.) No ....

9. Has your workers' education program a *faculty* advisory committee?
        Yes ....   No ....
  a. This committee has .... (number) members
  b. They come from   *(number)*
    1.) Liberal Arts College   ....
    2.) Graduate School   ....
    3.) College of Business Administration   ....
    4.) Extension Division   ....
    5.) School of Education   ....
    6.) Other divisions (specify)   ....
  c. By whom are members of this committee appointed?
  d. This committee meets
    1.) Quarterly   ....
    2.) Semiannually ....

3.) Annually ....
4.) Other stated intervals *(describe)*
e. This committee has a *stated* function?
   1.) Yes *(describe)* ....
   2.) No. ....

Finances

10. Your workers' education program gets its funds from:

	Appropriation	Length of fiscal period
a. Government	$.............	....
b. University	$.............	....
	Amount	
c. Fees	$.............	....

   1.) Fees levied

	Per student	Per group
a.) Consultation	$.............	$.............
b.) Classes	$.............	$.............
c.) Discussions		
1.) Lecture	$.............	$.............
2.) Film or filmstrip	$.............	$.............
d.) Conferences or institutes *(registration or tuition)*		
1.) Lodging *per night*	$.............	$.............
2.) Meals *per day*		
i.) Breakfast	$.............	$.............
ii.) Lunch	$.............	$.............
iii.) Dinner	$.............	$.............
e.) Other service *(describe)*	$.............	$.............

   2.) Costs *per activity:*

	From Appropriation	From Fees
a.) *Average* consultation	$.............	$.............
b.) *Average* class	$.............	$.............
c.) *Average* discussion		
1.) Lecture	$.............	$.............
2.) Film or filmstrip	$.............	$.............
d.) *Average* conference or institute (registration or tuition)	$.............	$.............
e.) Other service *(describe)*	$.............	$.............

Definition of function: relation to union educational programs

11. Check the statement below which *best explains* what your workers' education program considers to be its function.
...a. The function of the university in the present state of indus-

trial relations is to give organized labor educational facilities whereby it can satisfy those internal needs that will help build it to some degree of equality with industry. This means that the university should aim at equipping the worker with tools that will enable him to become a better wage-earner and a better union member.

The "understanding," and the "learning to know one another" that is expected between labor and management will then arise not in classroom contacts but around the conference table in contract negotiations. And there, too, will take place the ironing out of conflicting interests.

... b. Workers' education at our university:
    1.) Is *adult* education for *workers* on a *voluntary*, non-credit basis
    2.) Uses *informal* teaching techniques
    3.) Provides workers with a better understanding of their status, problems, rights and responsibilities *as workers, as union members, as consumers* and *as citizens.* (Will broaden their conceptual horizons, teach certain skills and/or train in the use of certain information.)
    4.) *Will lead to group action in solving* the above.

... c. The underlying assumption of a program of workers' education is that such specialized training will contribute to better industrial relations. Representatives of both labor and management should be brought together by the university in a common training program for mutual and cooperative analysis of the problems common to both groups. Such a common approach to these problems will bring greater understanding and appreciation of differing attitudes and will serve to narrow the areas in which conflicts of interest or disputes may arise in the future.

12. Does your workers' education program have in a written policy statement, brochure, pamphlet, etc., a definition of function?
    Yes ....   No ....
   a. If so, please return copy of that policy statement with this questionnaire.

13. Does your workers' education program have an *"understood" but not* written definition of function?
    Yes ....   No ....
   a. If so, please summarize.

14. Have labor organizations in the area which your workers' education program serves passed convention resolutions, meeting resolutions or given "testimonials" relative to that program?
    Yes ....   No ....
   a. If so, please return copies with this questionnaire or summarize *and identify sources.*

Types of Service

15. Does your workers' education program do specific research jobs for labor groups?
    Yes ....   No ....
    a. If so, please return illustrative example with this questionnaire.
16. Does your workers' education program conduct classes?
    Yes ....   No ....
    a. Where?
        1.) On-campus   ....
        2.) Off-campus   ....
            a.) Union halls   ....
            b.) Extension centers ....
            c.) Public schools   ....
            d.) Other buildings *(specify)*
    b. Class organization
        1.) Total number of sessions per course   ....
        2.) Frequency of sessions per week per course ....
        3.) Length of single session   ....
    c. Are classes conducted for:
        1.) Workers only   ....
        2.) Workers and management *together*   ....
        3.) Workers, management and the public *together* ....
        4.) Workers, management and public *separately*   ....
    d. How many classes did you conduct during your last fiscal year? *(number)* ....
    e. How many people did you serve through classes during your last fiscal year? *(number)* ....
    f. Please return a list of subjects your class program offers with this questionnaire.
17. Does your workers' education program conduct lecture or film discussions on either a single "spot" or series basis?
    Yes ....   No ....
    a. Where?
        1.) On-campus   ....
        2.) Off-campus   ....
            a.) Union halls   ....
            b.) Extension centers ....
            c.) Public schools   ....
            d.) Other buildings *(specify)*
    b. Are discussions conducted for:
        1.) Workers only   ....
        2.) Workers and management *together*   ....
        3.) Workers, management and the public *together* ....
        4.) Workers, management and public *separately*   ....

Appendix I
161

    c. How many discussions did you conduct during your last fiscal year? *(number)* ....
    d. How many people did you serve through discussions during your last fiscal year? *(number)* ....
    e. Please return a list of subjects your discussion program offers with this questionnaire.

18. Does your workers' education program conduct *off*-campus, year-round local or regional one-day or longer institutes or conferences
                    Yes ....   No ....
    a. Where?
       1.) Union halls   ....
       2.) Extension centers ....
       3.) Public schools   ....
       4.) Other buildings *(specify)*
    b. Are institutes and conferences conducted for:
       1.) Workers only   ....
       2.) Workers and management *together*   ....
       3.) Workers, management and the public *together* ....
       4.) Workers, management and the public *separately* ....
    c. How many institutes and conferences did you conduct during your last fiscal year? *(number)* ....
    d. How many people did you serve through institutes and conferences during your last fiscal year? *(number)* ....
    e. Please return illustrative institute or conference programs with this questionnaire.

19. Does your workers' education program conduct *on*-campus *summer* schools or institutes?
                    Yes ....   No ....
    a. Are *summer* programs conducted for:
       1.) Workers only   ....
       2.) Workers and management *together*   ....
       3.) Workers, management and the public *together* ....
       4.) Workers, management and the public *separately* ....
    b. How many *summer* programs did you conduct during your last fiscal year? *(number)* ....
    c. How many people did you serve through *summer* programs during your last fiscal year? *(number)* ....
    d. Please return illustrative *summer* school programs with this questionnaire.

Staff Organization

20. How many *full-time* people, *excluding director,* are employed by your workers' education program?
                  (number)
    a. Administrators   ....

b. Teachers ....
c. Secretarial ....
21. List the number of *administrators and teachers* on your staff whose *major* background is in each of the following areas.
    (number)
    a. Government ....
    b. Labor ....
    c. Management ....
    d. University ....
22. How many *part-time* people are employed by your workers 'education program?
    (number)
    a. Administrators ....
    b. Teachers ....
    c. Secretarial ....
23. List the number of part-time *teachers* on your staff who are *regularly employed elsewhere* in each of the following areas.
    (number)
    a. Government ....
    b. Labor ....
    c. Management ....
    d. Public School ....
    e. University ....
    f. Other *(specify)*
24. Check each of following qualifications *required* of part-time *teachers*.
    a. Experience in teaching adults ....
    b. Experience in labor movement ....
    c. A.B. degree ....
    d. M.A. degree ....
    e. Ph.D. degree ....
    f. Approval by faculty advisory committee ....
    g. Approval by workers' education program director ....
    h. Approval by administrator to whom workers' education program director responsible ....
25. What compensation *per hour* do you give part-time *teachers?*
26. Do you pay travel, food or lodging expense to part-time *teachers?*
    Yes ....   No ....
27. Check each of the following practices your *administrative staff* carries on.
    a. Regular observation of *teachers* ....

Appendix I

    b. Holding of *teaching staff* conferences   ....
        1.) Annually   ....
        2.) Semiannually   ....
        3.) Quarterly   ....
        4.) Other intervals ....
          (*describe*)

Supervision of Materials

28. Outlines or syllabi used in classes and discussions *must* be approved by:
    a. Lay advisory committee   ....
    b. Faculty advisory committee   ....
    c. Administrator to whom workers' education program director responsible   ....
    d. Workers' education program director   ....
    e. Teacher using them   ....

29. Books and pamphlets used in classes and discussions *must* have approval of:
    a. Lay advisory committee   ....
    b. Faculty advisory committee   ....
    c. Administrator to whom workers' education program director responsible   ....
    d. Workers' education program director   ....
    e. Teacher using them   ....

30. Audio-visual materials used in classes and discussions *must* have approval of:
    a. Lay advisory committee   ....
    b. Faculty advisory committee   ....
    c. Administrator to whom workers' education program director responsible   ....
    d. Workers' education program director   ....
    e. Teacher using them   ....

Liaison with Labor Movement

31. Does your workers' education program confer with appropriate national, regional and state labor officials on *overall program direction* as to:
    a. Subject matter
            Yes ....   No ....
    b. Teaching personnel
            Yes ....   No ....
    c. Teaching technique
            Yes ....   No ....

32. Does your workers' education program confer with appropriate labor officials on *a specific local program* as to:

a. Subject matter
   Yes ....   No ....
b. Teaching personnel
   Yes ....   No ....
c. Teaching technique
   Yes ....   No ....

33. Does your workers' education program arrange conference involving *at least* teacher assigned and responsible union scheduling officer, *before start* of a specific program, at which local interests and problems that program is designed to help satisfy or help solve are discussed?
   Yes ....   No ....

34. Does your workers' education program conduct conference, *at conclusion of a specific program,* at which that program is evaluated in terms of extent to which attempt to satisfy local interests and to solve local problems was successful?
   Yes ....   No ....
   a. Check people involved in such conferences
      1.) Teacher   ....
      2.) Workers' education program administrator   ....
      3.) Responsible union scheduling officer   ....
      4.) Students   ....

35. Does your workers' education program inform national, regional and local union education officers of what it is doing educationally with union members for whom those education officers are either directly or indirectly responsible?
   Yes ....   No ....
   a. This information is provided
      1.) Annually   ....
      2.) Semiannually ....
      3.) Quarterly   ....
      4.) Other stated intervals *(specify)*

36. Does your workers' education program aim at continual stimulation and strengthening of educational programs and facilities in unions themselves?
   Yes ....   No ....
   a. Do you maintain a consultation service for union educational personnel to further this aim?
      Yes ....   No ....

37. How do you initiate workers' educational activities you conduct?
   a. Await requests from unions   ....
   b. Circulate promotional literature   ....
   c. Staff members solicit unions by personal visits
      to officers and meetings   ....

Appendix I

SUPPLEMENTARY SURVEY QUESTIONNAIRE: Current Experiences of Colleges and Universities in Workers' Education

1. Has your college or university undergraduate or graduate programs in industrial relations which include curricula specifically designed to train for leadership or technical positions in the labor movement?
    Yes ....   No ....
    a. In what year were these programs initiated? ....
    b. Is there a direct relationship between your workers' education program and your undergraduate and graduate industrial relations program?
        Yes ....   No ....
        1.) If so, please describe.
    c. Total number of graduates of your industrial relations program since its inception ....
    d. Number of those graduates placed directly in the labor movement ....

Check list of materials you are asked to return with this questionnaire:

... 1. Question 12 — Copy of *written* policy statement
... 2. Question 14 — Copies of "testimonials"
... 3. Question 15 — Illustrative labor research job
... 4. Question 16 — List of courses offered
... 5. Question 17 — List of discussions offered
... 6. Question 18 — Illustrative conference or institute programs
... 7. Question 19 — Illustrative *summer* school programs

Please remember that promotional brochures, course outlines, syllabi and materials and any other materials you think may be helpful to this study will be appreciated.

Return them either with this questionnaire or under separate cover.

Appendix II: List of Colleges and Universities Surveyed

University of Akron, Akron, Ohio
  E. A. Tabler, Assistant Director, Division of Adult Education
University of Alabama,* University, Alabama
  J. R. Morton, Director, Continuation Education, Division of General Extension
Amherst College, Amherst, Massachusetts
  Colston E. Warne, Professor of Economics
Antioch College, Yellow Springs, Ohio
  Lewis Corey, Professor of Political Economy
University of Bridgeport,* Bridgeport, Connecticut
  Kenneth Hampson, Coordinator, Institute for Labor and Industrial Relations
University of California,* Berkeley, California
  Ronald W. Haughton, Assistant Director, Institute of Industrial Relations
University of California,* Los Angeles, California
  Arthur Carstens, Assistant Director of Community Relations, Institute of Industrial Relations
University of Chicago,*† Chicago, Illinois
  A. A. Liveright, Director, Union Programs and Union Leadership Training Project
University of Colorado, Boulder, Colorado
  Glenn S. Jensen, Administrative Assistant, Extension Division
University of Connecticut,*† Storrs, Connecticut
  John J. Glynn, Field Representative, Labor-Management Institute

---

* Questionnaire completed and returned.
† Program observed.

Appendix II

Cornell University,*† Ithaca, New York
  Ralph N. Campbell, Director of Extension, New York State School of Industrial and Labor Relations
University of Delaware, Newark, Delaware
  Charles N. Lanier, Chairman, Department of Economics and Business Administration
Duquesne University,* Pittsburgh, Pennsylvania
  Father George A. Harcar, Dean, School of Education
Fordham University,* New York, New York
  Philip A. Carey, S.J., Director Xavier Institute of Industrial Relations, College of St. Francis Xavier
Fresno State College, Fresno, California
  Victor L. Jepsen, Associate Professor of Business Administration
Goddard College,* Plainfield, Vermont
  A. R. Elliot, Jr., Director of Adult Education
Gonzaga University,* Spokane, Washington
  Clifford A. Carroll, S.J., Ph.D., Director, Industrial Relations Institute
Harvard University,*† Cambridge, Massachusetts
  James A. Healy, Director, Trade Union Program
Holy Cross College,* Worcester, Massachusetts
  Hubert C. Callaghan, S.J., Assistant Director, Institute of Industrial Relations
University of Illinois,*† Champaign, Illinois
  Phillips L. Garman, Coordinator of Extension, Institute of Labor and Industrial Relations
Indiana University,* Indianapolis, Indiana
  H. Fabian Underhill, Coordinator of Industrial Relations Programs, Division of Adult Education and Public Service
State University of Iowa, Iowa City, Iowa
  Fred J. Meyer, Assistant to the Director, Bureau of Labor and Management, College of Commerce
University of Kansas,* Lawrence, Kansas
  E. A. McFarland, Manager, Lawrence Center, University Extension Division
Kansas State College,* Manhattan, Kansas
  A. A. Holtz, Chairman, Department of Economics and Sociology
LeMoyne College,* Syracuse, New York
  Rev. Richard M. McKeon, S.J., Director, School of Industrial Relations

---

* Questionnaire completed and returned.
† Program observed.

Loyola University,* Los Angeles, California
  Rev. William J. McIntosh, S. J., Director, Industrial Relations School
Manhattan College,* New York, New York
  Brother C. Justin, F. S. C., Director, Westchester Labor School
Marquette University,* Milwaukee, Wisconsin
  Rev. C. N. McKinnon, S. J., Director, Marquette University Labor College
Marshall College,* Huntington, West Virginia
  E. S. Maclin, Director, Evening Program
University of Maryland, College Park, Maryland
  Harold F. Sylvester, Professor of Personnel Administration
Michigan State College, East Lansing, Michigan
  Charles C. Killingsworth, Head, Department of Economics
University of Minnesota,* Minneapolis, Minnesota
  Dale Yoder, Director, Industrial Relations Center, General Extension Division
Montana State University, Missoula, Montana
  Lucille Speer, Documents and Serials Librarian
University of New Hampshire,*† Durham, New Hampshire
  H. B. Stevens, Director, University Extension Service
Ohio State University,* Columbus, Ohio
  Glenn W. Miller, Associate Professor of Economics
Pennsylvania State College,*† State College, Pennsylvania
  Anthony Luchek, Head, Labor Education Service
Princeton University,† Princeton, New Jersey
  J. Douglas Brown, Director, Industrial Relations Section
University of Puerto Rico, San Juan, Puerto Rico
  Director, Institute of Labor Relations, School of Public Administration
Purdue University, Lafayette, Indiana
  C. H. Lawshe, Professor of Psychology
Rhode Island State College,*† Providence, Rhode Island
  Frederick G. Dunn, Supervisor, Workers Education Division, Division of General College Extension
Rockhurst College,* Kansas City, Missouri
  John C. Friedl, S. J., Director, Labor School Division, Institute of Social Order
Roosevelt College,*† Chicago, Illinois
  Frank W. McCallister, Director, Labor Education Division

---
* Questionnaire completed and returned.
† Program observed.

Appendix II

Rutgers University,*† The State University of New Jersey, New Brunswick, New Jersey
  Irvine L. H. Kerrison, Associate Professor in Charge, Labor Program, Institute of Management and Labor Relations
St. Joseph's College,*† Philadelphia, Pennsylvania
  Rev. Dennis J. Comey, S. J., Director, Institute of Industrial Relations
St. Peter's College,*† Jersey City, New Jersey
  Philip E. Dobson, S. J., Director, Institute of Industrial Relations
University of San Francisco,* San Francisco, California
  George E. Lucy, S. J., Director, Labor-Management School
University of Scranton,* Scranton, Pennsylvania
  Rev. James F. Dougherty, S. J., Director, Institute of Industrial Relations
University of Utah, Salt Lake City, Utah
  J. O. Horsfall, Director, Extension Division
University of Washington, Seattle, Washington
  Office of Short Courses and Conferences, University Extension Division
Washington University, St. Louis, Missouri
  William H. Reals, Dean, University College
Wayne University,† Detroit, Michigan
  Edward L. Cushman, Director, Institute of Industrial Relations
University of Wisconsin,* Madison, Wisconsin
  Vidkunn Ulriksson, Assistant Director, School for Workers
Yale University, New Haven, Connecticut
  Mary B. Clark, Executive Secretary, Labor and Management Center

---

* Questionnaire completed and returned.
† Program observed.

Appendix III: Workers' Education Directors Cooperating in Exchange of Materials

Miss Eleanor G. Coit, Director, American Labor Education Service, 1776 Broadway, New York 19, New York

Mr. Donald M. Irwin, Senior Extension Representative, Institute of Industrial Relations, University of California, Berkeley 4, California

Mr. Arthur Carstens, Research Associate, Institute of Industrial Relations, University of California, Los Angeles 24, California

Mr. A. A. Liveright, Director, Union Leadership Training Project, Industrial Relations Center, University of Chicago, Chicago 3, Illinois

Mr. George T. Guernsey, Associate Director of Education, Congress of Industrial Organizations, 718 Jackson Place, NW, Washington 6, D. C.

Miss Eleanor Emerson, New York State School of Industrial and Labor Relations, Cornell University, Ithaca, New York

Mr. Phillips L. Garman, Coordinator of Extension, Institute of Labor and Industrial Relations, University of Illinois, 704 South Sixth Street, Champaign, Illinois

Mr. Anthony Luchek, Head, Labor Education Service, Pennsylvania State College, State College, Pennsylvania

Mr. Frank McCallister, Director, Labor Education Division, Roosevelt College, 430 South Michigan Avenue, Chicago 5, Illinois

Mr. Irvine L. H. Kerrison, Associate Professor, Director of Labor Programs, Institute of Management and Labor Relations, Rutgers University, New Brunswick, New Jersey

Appendix III

Mr. Vidkunn Ulriksson, Assistant Director, School for Workers, University of Wisconsin, Madison 5, Wisconsin

Mr. John D. Connors, Director, Workers Education Bureau-AFL, 724 Ninth St., Washington, D. C.

Lists of workers' education materials furnished by the above cooperating agencies are prepared periodically by Ralph E. McCoy, Librarian, Institute of Labor and Industrial Relations, University of Illinois, 704 South Sixth Street, Champaign, Illinois

Appendix IV: First Summer Institute, International Chemical Workers Union—AFL Rutgers University, New Brunswick, N. J. July 10–15, 1950

Staff and Speakers:
(1) *Dr. Monroe Berkowitz,* Assistant Professor of Economics
College of Arts and Sciences, Rutgers University
(2) *H. A. Bradley,* President
International Chemical Workers Union–AFL
(3) *Gilbert Cain,* Assistant Safety Supervisor
Hercules Powder Company, Parlin, New Jersey
(4) *John D. Connors,* Director
Workers Education Bureau–AFL
(5) *Norman Dorfman,* Lecturer
Rutgers Institute of Management and Labor Relations
(6) *Arthur A. Elder,* Director, Training Institute
International Ladies' Garment Workers' Union–AFL
(7) *Dr. Bruce French,* Assistant Professor of Finance
University College, Rutgers University
(8) *Dr. Max Gideonse,* Chairman, Department of Economics
College of Arts and Sciences, Rutgers University
(9) *Dr. Irvine L. H. Kerrison,* In Charge, Labor Program
Rutgers Institute of Management and Labor Relations
(10) *Dr. Otto Pragan,* Research and Education Director
International Chemical Workers Union–AFL
(11) *Harry Stark,* Extension Associate, Labor Program
Rutgers Institute of Management and Labor Relations
(12) *Dr. Alberto Thompson,* Chief, Technical Information Branch
United States Atomic Energy Commission
(13) *R. E. Tomlinson,* Secretary-Treasurer
International Chemical Workers Union–AFL

Appendix IV

FIRST SUMMER INSTITUTE, INTERNATIONAL CHEMICAL WORKERS UNION–AFL

New Brunswick Campus; Rutgers, The State University of New Jersey; July 10–15, 1950

	MONDAY 10th	TUESDAY 11th	WEDNESDAY 12th	THURSDAY 13th	FRIDAY 14th	SATURDAY 15th
8:00–8:45 A.M.		Breakfast	Breakfast	Breakfast	Breakfast	Breakfast
9:00–10:30 A.M.	Registration (University Commons)	COLLECTIVE BARGAINING CLASS — Norman Dorfman (5)				
10:45–12:15 P.M.		PENSIONS AND WELFARE PLANS — Otto Pragan (10)			Economics of The Chemical Industry—Pragan	Wage Statistics Pragan
12:30–1:15 P.M.		Lunch	Lunch	Lunch	Lunch	Lunch—Where Do We Go From Here? —Pragan & Kerrison
1:30–3:00 P.M.		What Do We Mean By Unionism? Arthur A. Elder (6)	UNION ORGANIZATION AND ADMINISTRATION CLASS			
			History of ICW–AFL H. A. Bradley (2)	Financial Set-Up of ICW – R. E. Tomlinson (13)	Handling Executive Board and Membership Meetings Norman Dorfman	
3:15–4:30 P.M.		VISUAL MATERIALS WORKSHOP Irvine L. H. Kerrison (9)				CLASSES IN ROOM F
4:30–6:30 P.M.		PLANNED RECREATION			Bus Tour of Campus	Planned Recreation
6:30–7:30 P.M.		Dinner	Dinner	Dinner	Dinner	Dinner	MEALS IN ROOM E
7:45–9:15 P.M.	Political Education (film forum – "How A Bill Becomes A Law") Harry Stark (11)	Fair Deal Program (panel discussion) —John D. Connors, Chmn. (4). Monroe Berkowitz (1) Bruce French (7)	What About The Welfare State? Max Gideonse (8)	Safety in the Chemical Industry Gilbert Cain (3)	Atomic Power Alberto Thompson (12)	

Index

Adam, Thomas R., 5, 37, 107, 125
Adolfson, L. H., 129
Affiliated Schools for Workers, 15
Aiken, Senator George, 20
Akron, University of, 95
Alabama, University of, 94–95
Alderman, L. I., 15
Aldrich, Winthrop, 4
American Federation of Labor, 3, 6–7, 13, 19–26, 30, 39, 43, 49, 60–61, 84, 96, 99, 120, 127, 141, 144
American Federation of Teachers–AFL, 74, 97
Amherst College, 12, 94
Association of Land Grant Colleges, 24
Automobile Workers–CIO, United, 4, 31, 74, 92, 102

Bacon, Emery, 8
Bailey, Cleveland, 21
Barnard College, 91–92
Beck, Hubert P., 29
Biemiller, Andrew, 19
Bradley, Phillips, 35, 65
Brameld, Theodore, 62, 111
Bridgeport, University of, 57
Brookwood Labor College, 11–12
Brown, Leo C., 99
Bryce, James, 126
Bryn Mawr College, 11–12, 15
Bureau of National Affairs, 63

California, University of, 10–11, 40, 60, 93, 140

California State Federation of Labor, 11, 60, 108, 140
Campbell, Ralph N., 51
Carroll, Mollie Ray, 37, 106, 126
Chalmers, W. Ellison, 49
Chemical Workers Union–AFL, International, 102, 108
Chicago, University of, 49, 53, 63, 90–91, 108, 110, 128
Childs, John L., 33
Churchwomen, United Council of, 90
Cincinnati, University of, 12, 95
Clothing Workers Union–CIO, Amalgamated, 106
Cohn, Fannia, 4, 110
Colorado, University of, 96
Columbia University, 6–7, 12, 92, 114
Commission of Inquiry on the Workers Educational Service, 33–34
Congress, United States, 19–23
Congress of Industrial Organizations, 3, 6–7, 19–20, 43, 49, 61, 84, 96, 99, 102, 127, 144
Connecticut, University of, 93, 99
Connecticut Valley University Extension Committee, 94
Connors, John D., 7, 140–141
Cornell University, 17, 35, 38–40, 51, 56, 89, 95, 99, 108, 133
Counts, George E., 62, 111
Crane, William A., 33

175

Debatin, Frank, 41
Delaware, University of, 96
Detroit, University of, 92–93
Detroit Public Schools, 30
Dingwell, Robert, 4
Dix, Lester, 17
Douglas, Paul, 20
Dubinsky, David, 4
Dunlop, John, 105

Eby, Kermit, 7, 107, 126
Egbert, J. C., 12
Elder, Arthur A., 20, 31–32, 38, 107
Emerson, Lynn A., 38
Essert, Paul L., 6, 19, 36, 133

Federal Works Project, 77
Fernbach, A. P., 56
Fernbach, Frank, 126
Fisher, Winifred A., 33
Florida, University of, 41
Francis, Brother Felix, 92

General Motors Corporation, 21, 30–32, 35
Goddard College, 45, 76, 99
Gompers, Samuel, 120
Guernsey, George, 7–8, 141

Hallenbeck, Wilbur C., 114–115
Hansome, Marius, 30, 127
Harbison, Frederick B., 128
Hardman, J. B. S., 55, 106
Harvard University, 12, 53, 60, 78, 91–92, 105, 110
Healy, James J., 105
Herrmann, Lewis M., 60
Horne, Edmund, 92

Illinois, University of, 35, 40, 49, 57, 59, 63, 74, 93, 108, 113
Indiana University, 76
Iowa, The State University of, 95–96
Irving, Leonard, 20–21

Jacobs, Sam, 30–32
Jesus, Society of, 40, 45, 48, 53, 64, 71, 80
John Carroll University, 95
Johns Hopkins University, 9

Kefauver, Estes, 19
Keller, J. O., 24–25, 135
Kelsey, W. K., 32–33

Labor, United States Department of, 19–22, 107
Labor and Education, House Committee on, 20–21, 30
Labor and Public Welfare, Senate Committee on, 20, 24
Ladies' Garment Workers Union–AFL, International, 110–111
La Salle College, 92
Ligtenberg, John, 33
Lindeman, Eduard C., 40
Liveright, Alexander A., 49
Luchek, Anthony, 25, 49, 56
Lucy, George, 51

Machinists–AFL, International Association of, 49
Madden, Ray J., 20
Maryland, University of, 96
Massachusetts, University of, 94
Massachusetts Department of Education, 14
Massachusetts Institute of Technology, 12
Maurer, James H., 13
McCallister, Frank, 51
Michigan, University of, 20, 30–34, 39, 61, 92, 95–96, 125, 132
Michigan Bell Telephone Company, 32
Michigan CIO Council, 92
Michigan Committee on Civil Rights, 33
Michigan Federation of Teachers–AFL, 92
Michigan State College, 96
Michigan State Department of Public Instruction, 34, 96
Miller, Norman C., 13–14
Miller, Jr., Spencer, 7, 14–15, 18
Ming, William R., 33
Minnesota, University of, 63, 77–78, 93, 108, 113
Montana, University of, 96

INDEX

Morrill Act, 42
Morse, Wayne, 20
Mount Holyoke College, 94
Moyer, James A., 14

National Committee for the Extension of Labor Education, 24
National University Extension Association, 8–10, 12–15, 17, 24–26, 39, 41, 135
New Jersey State Federation of Labor–AFL, 15
Northeastern University, 95

Office of Price Administration, 30
Ohio State University, 76
Oklahoma, University of, 14, 95
Oklahoma State Federation of Labor, 14

Pennsylvania State College, 13, 25, 49, 56, 74, 108
Posey, Thomas E., 92
President's Advisory Committee on Education, 5
Puerto Rico, University of, 95–96

Quinn, Arthur, 14

Rhode Island State College, 58
Riley, B. C., 41
Roman Catholic Church, 45–46, 72
Roosevelt, Eleanor, 19
Roosevelt, Franklin D., 15
Roosevelt College, 51, 58, 91, 100, 110
Rutgers University, 14–15, 40, 51, 58, 60, 70, 74–76, 89, 93, 108, 113
Ruthven, Alexander G., 31–33

St. Joseph's College, 57
St. Michael's College, 95
San Francisco, University of, 51
Schwarztrauber, Ernest E., 55, 76, 89, 124, 132, 135
Seafarers' International Union–AFL, 74
Sigler, Kim, 32
Sill, Charles, 32

Smith, Hilda W., 12, 15, 121
Smith College, 94
Soop, Everett J., 32
Starr, Mark, 96–97, 105, 110
Steelworkers of America–CIO, United, 8, 76, 90, 95, 108
Stricker, Jr., Adam K., 30–32
Syracuse University, 12

Textile Workers Union–CIO, 74
Thomas, Elbert D., 20
Toledo, University of, 94
Tollefson, Thor C., 20
Trade Union College of Boston, 12
Truman, Harry S., 21
Tufts College, 12
Typographical Union–AFL, International, 60

Ulriksson, Vidkunn, 49
United Negro College Fund, 4
Utah, University of, 95
Utah State Federation of Labor–AFL, 95

Virginia, University of, 41, 56

Washington University, 41, 96
Wayne University, 30, 96
West Virginia State College, 92
Williams, Mennen G., 34
Wilson, C. E., 31
Wirtenberger, Henry J., 92–93, 99
Wisconsin, University of, 5, 49, 76, 88–89, 92, 129, 132
Witte, Edwin, 5, 35
Women's Trade Union League, 12
Woodward High School, 12
Work Projects Administration, 15–19
Workers Education Bureau, 7, 11–13, 15, 41, 43, 102, 107
Workers Educational Association, 11, 14, 123, 137

Yale University, 90, 108, 113

Zehmer, George B., 41